# NO FREE ATTENTION

## How Women use **The Possibility of Sex** to Manipulate Naïve and Lustful Men

**ALAN ROGER CURRIE**

**Mode One Multimedia, Inc.**
http://directapproachdating.com
coaching@modeone.net

ISBN: 978-1-7361951-2-3



Printed on acid-free paper.

Mode One Multimedia, Inc.
2021

Library of Congress Cataloguing in Publication Data
Currie, Alan Roger
No FREE Attention: How Women use The Possibility of Sex to Manipulate Naïve and Lustful Men by Alan Roger Currie
Library of Congress Control Number: 2020921939

Website: **http://directapproachdating.com**
Coaching: **http://patreon.com/modeone**

Other eBooks, paperbacks, and audiobooks published by Author Alan Roger Currie:

***Mode One: Let the Women Know What You're REALLY Thinking***

***Mode One – HARDCORE*** *(eBook only)*

***Upfront and Straightforward: Let the Manipulative Game Players Know What You're REALLY Thinking***

***Mode One – Semantics and Scenarios: Inside the Mind of the Manipulative Game Player*** *(eBook only)*

***Oooooh . . . Say it Again: Mastering the Fine Art of Verbal Seduction and Aural Sex***

***The Beta Male Revolution: Why Many Men Have Totally Lost Interest in Marriage in Today's Society***

# NO FREE ATTENTION

How Women use **The Possibility of Sex** to Manipulate Naïve and Lustful Men

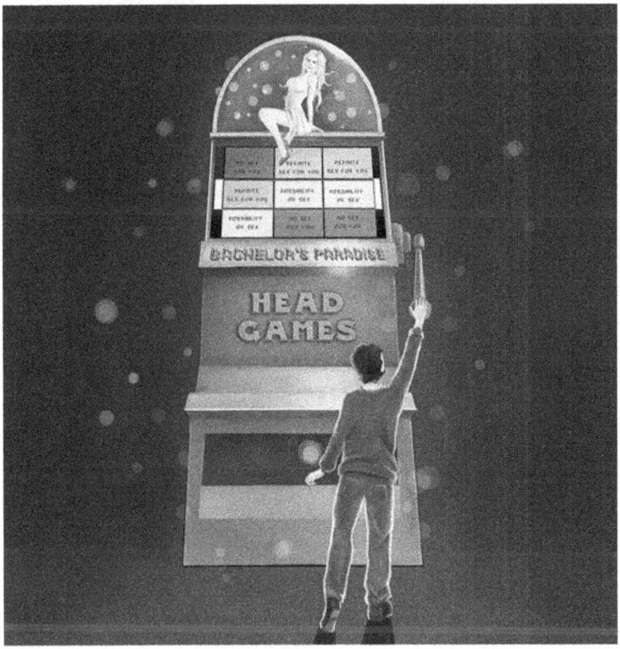


**ALAN ROGER CURRIE**

MODE ONE

**Mode One Multimedia, Inc.**
http://directapproachdating.com
coaching@modeone.net

# Table of Contents

# Introduction & Acknowledgements

Of my four major books that are now published eBooks and audiobooks, this book is the only one that had not yet been published as a paperback. Also, if you noticed, I modified the title a bit. When I originally published this as an eBook in 2012, and later as an audiobook in 2014, the title was ***The Possibility of Sex: How Naïve and Lustful Men are Manipulated by Women Regularly***.

If you currently own either my 2012 eBook and/or my 2014 audiobook, you already know that arguably the most popular concept that was espoused in each of those two versions was my personal philosophy of "**No Free Attention**," which represented my belief that no single heterosexual man should ever give a woman full and indefinite access to his **non-sexual** time, attention, and companionship unless . . .

A) He and his designated woman of interest are currently engaging in sexual relations;

B) He is not yet engaging in sexual relations with his designated woman of interest, but she has made it crystal clear that she is very much interested in engaging in sexual relations with him in the very near future;

C) The woman has made it clear that she is not at all interested in engaging in sexual relations with the man, but the man is more so genuinely interested in socially interacting with the woman in a purely platonic manner and/or he is interacting with her in a manner that will prove to be beneficial to him career-wise, financially, or socially.

Beginning with no later than 2015, I began to observe a lot of other professional dating coaches, pickup artists (PUAs), and other assorted "self-improvement gurus" adopting my concept of "**No Free Attention**" without giving me my proper credit attribution for popularizing the concept.

I have been operating with the *No Free Attention* philosophy since March 1988, which is before many of the men who are currently active in what is known as "The Manosphere" **were even born**.

For example, just earlier this year, I had a young PUA type who is based in Miami upload a video on YouTube titled "No Free Attention for Women!" I wrote him and said, "FYI: You know I popularized the phrase 'No Free Attention' don't you?? You did not give me any credit for it in your video." He initially replied, *"Well, with all due respect to you Alan, I have been using the phrase 'no free attention' since like 2017. Maybe even 2016."*

I quickly let him know that I had been using that phrase and philosophy since 1988, and then he was like, *"Holy shit! Wow! 1988?!?!? Wow! Sorry Alan. I had no idea that you had been using that phrase and philosophy for **that long**. If that is the case, then you are pretty much the originator of that concept then. You are indeed The Godfather!"*

Actually, one of my top two nicknames among men in what is known as *The Manosphere* is "**The Godfather of Direct (Verbal) Game Advice & Wisdom**." I have literally lost count of the number of other dating coaches, PUAs, and self-proclaimed "self-improvement gurus" or "seduction gurus" who have borrowed talking points from one or more of my books without giving me what is known as "**Proper Credit Attribution**."

For those who may not be aware of this long-standing tradition, anytime you repeat and regurgitate other published authors' unique terms, signature phrases, original concepts, and direct quotes and personal philosophies, you are always supposed to give ***proper credit attribution*** to the author(s) whose material and intellectual property you are borrowing talking points and material from. If you fail to do this, then technically you are guilty of **plagiarism** and/or **copyright infringement**.

All that to say, the main reason why I modified the title of this book from ***The Possibility of Sex*** to ***No Free Attention*** is because I want all the men (and women) who read this book to know that I am the dating coach and author **who first popularized** this concept, signature phrase, and personal philosophy. Anytime you hear another dating coach, PUA, or self-improvement guru use the phrase "**No Free Attention**," trust me … they borrowed it *(or flat-out STOLE IT)* from **ME**.

Secondly, in full disclosure, this is not really a 'stand-alone' book. This book is actually part of what I would loosely refer to as a "trilogy" of books. If I had to use the Star Wars® movies as a lighthearted analogy, the first book in the trilogy, ***Mode One***, is like Star Wars, Episode IV; the second book in the trilogy, ***Oooooh … Say it Again***, is like Star Wars, Episode V; and this book, ***No Free Attention / The Possibility of Sex***, is like Star Wars, Episode VI. Then, I would refer to my book titled ***The Beta Male Revolution*** as "The Prequel" to my designated 'trilogy' *(similar to Star Wars, Episodes I, II, and III)*.

I do not really view ***Mode One***, ***Oooooh … Say it Again***, and ***No Free Attention / The Possibility of Sex*** as three (3) separate books. I more so view all three as **ONE LONG BOOK** divided into three (3) separate parts.

Finally, I would like to offer an enthusiastic shout-out to my brother, Stephen Clarence Currie; my wife, Jameelah Currie; Alix Edouard Grand-Pierre and Alvin Hollinger III, who both first encouraged me to write and publish my 2012 eBook version of this book; Esther Vilar, whose popular best-selling book, *The Manipulated Man* was a partial inspiration and influence for my own book; and the late, great adult film actor John Leslie, whose fictional character of the prolific womanizer "Jack" in the 1980 adult film, *Talk Dirty to Me*, was my first major inspiration for my entire **Mode One** philosophy.

## The Primary Basis for My MODE ONE Philosophy

When it comes to single heterosexual men attempting to connect with women either for **a)** long-term, strictly monogamous sex, **b)** long-term, non-monogamous *(i.e., polygamy or polyamory)* sex, **c)** short-term, strictly monogamous sex *(i.e., "serial monogamy")*, or **d)** short-term, non-monogamous sex *(i.e., promiscuous casual sex)*, I tend to place all women in five different 'archetypes' as far as their verbal communication style:

**Reciprocators** – These are women that once a man verbally communicates his romantic or strictly sexual desires, interests, and intentions to a woman, this woman will quickly, straightforwardly, and enthusiastically reciprocate his desires & interests;

**Rejecters** – These are women that once a man verbally communicates his romantic or strictly sexual desires, interests, and intentions to a woman, this woman will quickly and straightforwardly convey to the man that she has absolutely no interest in sharing his company in any sort of physically intimate manner;

**Wholesome Pretenders** – These are women that once a man verbally communicates his desire to engage in one or more episodes of short-term non-monogamous 'casual' sex, this woman will **INITIALLY** behave as though she is 'turned off' or simply 'not interested,' but in reality, this woman is open to being *persuaded* and *seduced* into engaging in one or more episodes of casual sex with a man;

**Erotic Hypocrites** – These are women that are a more pretentious, materialistic, and antagonistic & argumentative variation of a *Wholesome Pretender* type. These are women who more or less operate as "covert Call Girls" who seek to receive monetary favors and materialistic gifts from men in direct exchange for their (short-term, non-monogamous) sexual companionship;

**Manipulative Timewasters** – These are women that once a man verbally communicates his romantic or strictly sexual desires, interests, and intentions to a woman, this woman will TEMPORARILY or INDEFINITELY seek to give a man ***the very misleading impression*** that she is genuinely interested in sharing his company in some sort of physically intimate manner, but in reality, this woman is just seeking to maintain a purely platonic friendship with a man and/or exploit a man for his financial resources and material possessions.

My book, ***Mode One***, offers the basic framework for explaining to men why **direct verbal communication** is much more effective toward the objective of quickly identifying *Wholesome Pretender* types, *Erotic Hypocrite* types, and *Manipulative Timewaster* types compared to using some variation of <u>indirect</u> verbal communication (i.e., **Mode Two** and/or **Mode Three** verbal communication styles).

My book, ***Oooooh … Say it Again***, is the book that exclusively focuses on the two sexually duplicitous archetypes of women, which would be the *Wholesome Pretender* types and the *Erotic Hypocrite* types, and it explains how a man can use his **verbal seduction skills** and his **erotic dirty talk talents** to charm and persuade these two types of women into engaging in one or more episodes of short-term, non-monogamous 'casual' sex with him.

Finally, this book … ***No FREE Attention / The Possibility of Sex*** … centers on helping men quickly and effectively identify women who are a combination of **dishonest**, **disingenuous**, **misleading & manipulative**, and generally **materialistic**. In other words, what I refer to as the *Manipulative Timewaster* types of the world.

Just months ago, I had a follower and supporter of mine express to me that he viewed me as a one of the premiere thought leaders and pioneers of *The Manosphere*, and that my knowledge, wisdom, insight, and overall advice contributed to him experiencing a high number of personal epiphanies and modifying a good number of his long-standing paradigms and beliefs regarding the general nature of socially interacting with women, and pursuing them for romantic and/or strictly sexual companionship.

I will refer to this follower and supporter as "Frank" (not his real first name), and Frank highlighted at least three major areas where I helped him view interactions with women very differently:

1) Frank said that before becoming familiar with my books, he used to believe that bringing up the subject of sex in your very first conversation with a woman of interest was a huge "No No." Frank had been taught by his mother, his older brother, and various friends and social acquaintances that discussing anything related to his sexual desires, interests, and intentions with women in his **very first conversation with them** would cause a woman to feel disrespected, insulted, offended, and generally 'turned off.' Frank said that my books, ***Mode One*** and ***Oooooh … Say it Again*** totally changed his mind regarding his original belief and attitude about this;

2) Frank said that before he became familiar with my books, he used to believe that the most effective way to motivate a woman to engage in one or more episodes of short-term and/or non-monogamous sex was to exhibit behavior that is dishonest, disingenuous and misleading, and generally manipulative *(i.e., this is what I refer to as **Mode Three** Behavior)*, or at bare minimum, engage in a conversation style with women that was very pleasant, polite, cautious, flattering, entertaining, and vague & ambiguous *(i.e., this is what I refer to as **Mode Two** Behavior)*. Frank said it was not until he read both ***Mode One*** and ***Oooooh … Say it Again*** that he realized all of the major detriments, flaws, weaknesses, and general drawbacks to employing either *Mode Two* and/or *Mode Three* Behavior with women, and that exhibiting a *Mode One direct verbal communication style with women* was much more conducive to his needs and objectives in the long-run;

3) Finally, Frank expressed to me that because of many years of following the advice of multiple conventional PUAs and other dating coaches, Frank had always believed that if a woman smiled at him, engaged in friendly

> and flirtatious conversations with him, and she agreed to join him on a number of lunch dates, dinner dates, movie dates, and other types of 'dates,' that this meant that 90 - 99% chance, the woman was genuinely interested in sharing his company at some point in the future in a romantic or strictly sexual manner. It was not until Frank **a)** found himself wasting a lot of **time** and **money** on a high number of women without any of his investments of both ever leading to sexual intimacy with these women and **b)** read my book, ***The Possibility of Sex*** that he fully realized that not *every* woman who appears to give a man "indicators of interests" (IOIs) and/or "choosing signals" *(both of these are conventional PUA terms)* is genuinely interested in engaging in sexual relations with that man. In a nutshell, Frank said that before coming across my material, he had **NO IDEA** that women who operate as ***Manipulative Timewasters*** even existed.

Frank said that none of the conventional PUAs that he followed ever even remotely mentioned an archetype of women similar to *Manipulative Timewasters*. This does not surprise me even one bit.

From a strictly **business standpoint**, I totally understand why the vast majority of conventional PUAs do not want men to know about the archetype of women who I refer to as *Manipulative Timewasters*.

You see, conventional PUAs earn money from clients by giving (naïve and impressionable) men the misleading impression that their advice will lead to their clients a) becoming some sort of 'overnight ladies' man' and 'overnight womanizer,' and secondly, b) that their advice will directly lead to men being able to significantly diminish their instances of quick, abrupt, straightforward, and harsh rejection from women.

One of ways that conventional PUAs accomplish the "b" objective is by giving men the very invalid and misleading impression that if the man is able to 1) prevent and avoid any and all **negative reactions and responses from women** and 2) provoke a woman to interact with him in a very **enthusiastic**, **friendly**, and more so **flirtatious** manner, that nine times out of ten, he will eventually get that woman to agree to engage in sexual relations with him.

In reality, nothing could be further from the truth.

Think about it. If all a man had to do in order to get a woman to agree to have sex with him is to maintain a conversation style that was "pleasant," "polite," "friendly," flattering & entertaining, and generally representative of a well-mannered 'innocent flirt,' then every man who fancies himself a "classy gentleman" and the proverbial "nice guy" would never, ever experience any challenges or problems getting women in bed.

Here is the hardcore truth about women:

1) Not all women who are interested in engaging in sexual relations with a man *(and particularly, some form of short-term and/or non-monogamous sex)* are going to verbally communicate those desires to men in an upfront, genuine, and straightforwardly honest manner. Among other reasons, the vast majority of women are too paranoid about anything that is going to negatively affect their **public image** and **social reputation** (in blunt terms, no woman wants to develop a reputation for being a 'whore' and/or a 'slut'). This is why you have the two archetypes of women that I refer to as *Wholesome Pretenders* and *Erotic Hypocrites* (I discuss these archetypes in more specific detail in my book titled ***Oooooh … Say it Again***)

2) Similar to #1, not all women who are **NOT INTERESTED** in either dating a man long-term or engaging in 'casual' sexual relations with a man short-term are going to verbally communicate their lack of interest to men in an upfront, unapologetic, and straightforwardly honest manner. Why not? For starters, **many women are afraid of being physically assaulted** by men as a direct result of abruptly or harshly rejecting a man. I have had literally hundreds of women convey this sentiment to me over the last thirty-five years. Just last year, there was a college student in Chicago who was murdered because a man became angry when she rebuffed his sexual advances. Secondly, many women want to exploit men who they know have a strong desire to engage in sexual relations with them so that they can a) gain full and indefinite access to that man's **non-sexual** time, attention, and companionship and/or b) take advantage of that man's financial resources and overall sense of financial & materialistic generosity.

The latter part of #2, in simple terms, is why you have women who operate as *Manipulative Timewasters*. These women have absolutely **no interest** in your **sexual** attention and companionship, but they are extremely interested in some specific aspect of your **non-sexual** time, attention, and companionship.

You see, most of these women are **very savvy**. *Manipulative Timewasters* know that if they let you know too quickly and/or too straightforwardly that they have zero interest in engaging in sexual relations with you, that you are never going to invest any significant amount of **time** and/or **money** pursuing their romantic or strictly sexual companionship.

This is why a man's **verbal communication style** is so important. When a man verbally communicates his romantic or strictly sexual desires, interests, and intentions to a woman in a highly self-assured, upfront, very specific, and straightforwardly honest manner (i.e., he exhibits what I refer to as ***Mode One*** Behavior with women), then he places a woman in a position where she only has one of two options: either a) fully reciprocate the man's desires & interests, or b) straightforwardly reject the man's desires & interests.

The problem with the vast majority of men is that they LOVE reaction "a," but they HATE receiving a "b" response.

The vast majority of men cannot handle being abruptly and straightforwardly rejected by a woman who they find very physically attractive and sexually appealing. Most men will attempt to do damn near anything to prevent themselves from being rejected by a woman of interest.

Many men will **excessively flatter** women in an attempt to avoid being rejected.

Many men will go out of their way to **entertain** women and **make them smile, giggle, and/or laugh** in an attempt to avoid being rejected.

Many men will offer women **free meals, monetary favors, and materialistic gifts** in an attempt to avoid being rejected.

Many men will temporarily or indefinitely **pretend as though they are content with being a woman's purely platonic friend** in an attempt to avoid being rejected.

And in a worst-case scenario, some men will resort to **raping or date-raping** a woman to avoid being denied the opportunity to engage in sexual relations with a woman.

In the next five chapters, I going to cover each of those five attempts to prevent and avoid rejection one by one in more specific detail.

Here is the bottom line, that most men do not realize: When you resort to the first four of those five attempts to prevent and avoid rejection *(i.e., flattering women regularly and excessively, providing women with humorous and highly entertaining conversation, offering women free meals, monetary favors, and materialistic gifts, and pretending to be content with being a woman's purely platonic male friend)*, **you very much open yourself up to being easily and frequently manipulated by women who are *Manipulative Timewaster* types.**

Even worse, if you resort to some form of sexual assault *(e.g., groping women, forcing yourself on women, date-raping or raping women, et al)*, you will soon be looking to enter into prison at some point in the very near future, and gain the opportunity to share a cell with "Big Bubba" who loves man butt.

Continue reading my friend.

# PART ONE

## Men Who Seek to Excessively Flatter Women in order to Win Favor with Them

The first of the **5 types of men** who I am going to discuss who go out of their way to prevent and avoid being rejected by women and hopefully prevent and avoid any and all forms of 'negative' reactions and responses from women are men who resort to regularly and/or excessively **flattering women**. I generally refer to these types of men as ***Ego Boosters & Self-Esteem Boosters*** for women.

I have never met a woman in my life who does not enjoy being complimented. Women love receiving flattering comments from men that validate their sense of beauty and physical sex appeal as well as a number of their non-physical and non-sexual attributes and qualities.

There are some women who literally become 'addicted' to flattering attention from men. I am talking, they cannot live without it. Flattering attention becomes as desirable to them as oxygen, food and water, and/or money.

Put bluntly, many women place the same value on **flattering attention** and **entertaining conversation** *(which I will cover in the very next chapter)* that many men place on sexual enjoyment and satisfaction.

For example, many women who post photos of themselves on social media (such as Instagram) of them adorned in swimwear or lingerie. These women just want a heavy dose of flattering attention from (horny) men.

I remember back in the 1980s, I used to ride a commuter train from the Miller Beach neighborhood of Gary, Indiana to Chicago in the morning and then back from Chicago to Miller Beach in late afternoon or early evening.

During one stretch of a few months, there was this one particular African American woman who would always choose to sit next to me. One time she came and took a seat next to me while I was reading a newspaper. Within minutes, she became highly agitated. I asked, "What is wrong with you? Is everything okay?" Initially she responded, *"Oh, nothing. I am fine."* Then she kept behaving more and more as if she was really irritated about something. She kept fidgeting in her seat in a very blatant manner. So again, I asked her, "Is everything alright?" For the second time, she said that she was fine.

Finally, after approximately ten minutes had passed, she said, *"Okay Alan, I am going to be very, very honest with you."* I replied, "Okay ... what is on your mind? Be real. Be one-hundred percent honest with me."

She said, *"Alan, I don't like it when you sit next to me and you don't say anything to me. I hate it when you are consumed with reading newspapers and magazines while I am seated next to you."* Half of me was somewhat surprised to hear her say that, but knowing female nature the way I do, I was not totally surprised.

She continued with, *"Being blunt, I hate to be ignored by men. I hate it when men are silent for too long when they are in my presence. I want a man to talk to me, flatter me, and entertain me. I want him to share with me how attractive he thinks I am and how sexy he feels I am. If a man goes too long without doing those things, I become irritated. Is that honest enough for you?"*

Not only do many women who are single and unattached frequently fall into this category, but many women who are married, engaged to be married, or otherwise romantically involved with a man seek to be flattered and entertained by men who they have no interest in dating or engaging in casual sex with.

As you continue with your life as a man, the one thing you need to always keep in mind about women is that women live to be flattered and entertained, and made to feel as though they are physically attractive, sexually desirable, and generally enjoyable to be around.

You see, men - generally speaking - are different. Men are wired differently than women are. Men do not get off on receiving compliments about their physical appearance or live to receive egotistical flattery and engage in entertaining conversations with women.

The main thing most men want from women *(assuming they are heterosexual, or at least bisexual)* is the opportunity to be physically intimate with them. Kiss them, make out with them, and eventually engage in oral sex and/or vaginal intercourse with them.

I want to make something very clear: All women who are *Manipulative Timewaster* types love and seek out flattering attention, but not all women who love and seek out flattering attention from men are *Manipulative Timewasters*.

In other words, if a woman makes it known to you from the beginning of your social interactions with her that she has absolutely no interest in becoming your future wife, your next long-term girlfriend, or your next brand new casual sex lover, then that woman cannot be branded as or validly categorized as a *Manipulative Timewaster*.

To reiterate, a *Manipulative Timewaster* is a woman that will mislead a man into believing that if he continues to behave in a manner that is pleasing to her, and he continues to perform financial and non-financial favors for her, that she will ultimately 'reward' him with one or more opportunities to engage in sexual relations with her … even though she knows deep down that she will **NEVER, EVER** allow that man to engage in sexual relations with her.

A man who is not afraid of being rejected by a woman will have no problem verbally communicating his romantic or strictly sexual desires, interests, and intentions to a woman in a ***Mode One*** manner. This type of man will usually be able to quickly identify and effectively weed out women who are *Manipulative Timewaster* types within the first ten-to-fifteen minutes of their very first conversation with a woman.

On the other hand, if you are a man who hates the idea of being abruptly and straightforwardly rejected by a woman, or similarly, you hate being harshly criticized and insulted by women in response to the things you say and do, then you will always be ideal prey for a woman who is a *Manipulative Timewaster*. Always.

Many men foolishly believe that if they regularly or semi-regularly flatter women to the highest degree, and generally operate as a woman's personal *Ego Booster & Self-Esteem Booster*, they are going to earn some sort of valuable "Brownie Points" that they will be able to cash in at a later date for an opportunity to engage in sexual relations with a woman.

Any woman who is a *Manipulative Timewaster* type that specifically seeks out men to become her personal *Ego Booster & Self-Esteem Booster* for a period of days, weeks, months, or even years is generally known in society as a "Whore for Flattering Attention," or for short, simply an *Attention Whore*.

As I alluded to already, various **social media** platforms *(e.g., Instagram, Facebook, etc.)* are full of women who are *Attention Whore* types. Many women know that if they upload a photo and/or video of themselves wearing something short, tight, revealing, and/or sexually provocative in general, that they will have dozens, hundreds, or even possibly thousands of (horny) men enthusiastically ready to shower them with flattering compliments on a daily, weekly, or monthly basis.

Rarely if ever do I offer women an "empty compliment." What exactly is an *empty compliment*?

If you were to approach a woman, initiate a conversation with her, and immediately say something such as, "You are SO beautiful!!" or "You are SO sexy!!" ... but then, after expressing such a compliment, you said NOTHING ELSE to follow up that compliment ... and the woman simply says, *"Why, THANK YOU!! You are so kind!"* and then quietly walks away ... that would be representative of an ***empty compliment***.

Beginning with no later than the age of 21 or 22, 99% of my compliments to women have been **action-oriented compliments**.

An *action-oriented compliment* is when you follow-up a compliment by expressing to a woman that you desire to share her company at some point in the near future, and even more so, you let the woman know specifically WHY you desire to share her company.

All men who exhibit ***Mode One*** Behavior with women utilize *action-oriented compliments*. On the other hand, men who frequently exhibit some variation of ***Mode Two*** and/or ***Mode Three***

Behavior with women generally tend to express a lot of empty compliments.

Empty compliment: ***"I have to tell you … you have some very beautiful eyes and some very nice lips!"***

Action-oriented compliment: ***"Your eyes are beautiful, and your lips are very sexy … and I look forward to looking directly into your eyes right before I tongue-kiss you at some point in the near future. When would you like to share my company one-on-one … next Friday, or next Saturday? "***

See the difference?

If you offer an empty compliment to a *Manipulative Timewaster* type, you are playing right into her hands. Women who are *Manipulative Timewaster* types live to receive a wide assortment of *empty compliments* from a multiplicity of (horny) heterosexual (and even bisexual) men.

I have known women in my life that regularly maintained at least a dozen or more men in their social circle just to operate as *Ego Boosters* and *Self-Esteem Boosters* for them.

Once a woman has you tabbed as an *Ego Booster & Self-Esteem Booster*, there is a 99.999% chance that you are never, ever going to end up engaging in sexual relations with that woman. Why would any woman feel motivated to allow you to have sex with her, when she can receive flattery and egotistical validation from you **FOR FREE**.

If you are a man who falls into this category in your social interactions with women, I know for a fact that you have wasted many hours, days, weeks, months, and even years excessively flattering women's egos only to remain in their dreaded *"we're just friends only"* category. Be honest.

Quit offering women *empty compliments*. From this day forward, concentrate on only offering women ***action-oriented compliments***. Soon, you will see your love life, sex life, and overall social life improve. At bare minimum, you will be able to quickly identify and effectively weed out all the women in your life that are nothing more than a *Manipulative Timewaster*.

If there is one habit that is just as bad as offering women too many *flattering empty compliments*, **it is engaging in way too much trivial, but highly entertaining conversations with women**.

This is what I am going to discuss in the very next chapter.

Continue reading my friend.

# Men Who Seek to Entertain Women and/or Engage in Very Trivial 'Small Talk' in order to Win Favor with Them

If anyone owns either the 1999 eBook version of my ***Mode One*** book and/or the 2006 paperback version of ***Mode One***, they will recall that my very first sentence in Chapter One of that book is *"I hate trivial chit chat, fluff talk, and small talk."*

If you visit Amazon.com right now, you will probably find at least a dozen books that encourage men and women to engage in trivial, but entertaining *chit chat*, *fluff talk*, and *small talk*. If such behavior is the 'rule,' consider me the 'exception to the rule.'

***Small talk*** is any form of conversation that you engage in with others that has no bearing on you finding out more important and relevant personal information about them, and it does nothing to help you determine if you are genuinely compatible with this person.

In this chapter, I am going to focus on the second of the **5 types of men** who seek to prevent and avoid rejection from women as much as possible, and I refer to these men as women's ***Personal (Comedic) Entertainers*** who provide women with very humorous and entertaining conversation on a regular or semi-regular basis.

If you own the original 2012 eBook version or the 2014 audiobook version of ***The Possibility of Sex,*** you'll know that it is this category of men that first provoked me developing the concept and maintaining the personal philosophy of **NO FREE ATTENTION** back in the late 1980s.

Without getting too lengthy with the backstory, I used to have a very bad habit of engaging in at least a few minutes of entertaining conversations with women just for the heck of it. I always had a reputation for being funny *(I actually was once a professional standup comedian in 1989 and 1990)*, and I usually got a kick out of making women laugh, particularly when I was in the workplace.

The problem that arose from this was that the vast majority of women who I would engage in these very humorous, highly entertaining conversations with hardly ever ended up having sex with me. I usually ended up in these co-worker's "friend zone."

The one experience that changed me was when I worked with a man in Downtown Chicago in Spring 1988. His name was Anthony *(I cannot recall his last name)*, and it was Anthony who first passed on the infamous concept to me of not giving female co-workers or female business colleagues any sort of "free" attention.

Anthony sort of resembled the late, great Charlie Murphy *(Comedian and Movie Star Eddie Murphy's older brother who achieved fame on "The Dave Chappelle Show")*, and within the company that he and I worked for in 1988, Anthony had a reputation for being extremely aloof, standoffish, and unresponsive when it came to engaging in trivial *chit chat*, *fluff talk*, *small talk*, and even momentary *'social pleasantries'* with our female co-workers.

Now even before I met Anthony, I was never the biggest fan of *small talk* and the like, but many times, I would engage in at least maybe two, three, four, or five minutes' worth of *social pleasantries* with women, and in particular female co-workers and female business colleagues. Not Anthony.

In blunt terms, Anthony would not talk to our female co-workers **at all** in any type of non-work related and/or purely social manner. I mean, he would not say anything to them. Not even a *"Hello there Barbara ... how are you this morning?"* or *"Hey Janet, how was your weekend? I hope it was relaxing and enjoyable."* Anthony would not say JACK to women once he arrived into the workplace to perform his professional duties.

As a result, the response he received from the women in our workplace was mixed. On one end, a lot of our female co-workers were irritated by his total lack of desire to engage in trivial but entertaining *small talk* and *social pleasantries* with them … but at the same time, it seemed to motivate quite a few of our female co-workers to become a bit more aggressive in seeking out opportunities to engage in conversation with him and they would make multiple attempts to gain access to his **non-sexual attention and companionship** while we were at work. Observing this left me intrigued.

So, one day in March 1988, I initiated a conversation with Anthony in the company's break room. I lightheartedly asked him, "Hey brother … what is your secret for getting these women to basically 'beg you' for your attention?" Initially, he just casually glared at me. He possessed this facial expression that sent the message to me, *"What makes you think you have the right to ask me questions? I don't know you man."*

Then, after receiving no response, I became persistent and asked him the same question a second time. After a few moments of silence, he finally responded with, *"I don't believe in giving women free attention like you do."* I was like, "Free attention? What do you mean by that?" Anthony went on to explain, *"I only talk to these women here at work if I absolutely, positively have to. For example, asking a woman a question to retrieve information that is going to help me do my job better. Other than that, I don't have anything to say to these women here at work. If me and a woman are not fucking or doing business together, then I really don't have shit to say to that woman.* ***I am never going to talk to a woman just to entertain her or make her laugh or make her feel comfortable in my presence****. Again, I don't give women any of my (non-sexual) attention for* ***free****. If me and a woman are fucking, or doing business and making money together, then I will talk to her. Otherwise, I have nothing to say to her. Nothing."*

Realistically, I am probably still not as hardline as my former co-worker Anthony was back in 1988, but after that conversation with him that day in the break room, that is when I first began adopting the personal philosophy of ***no free non-sexual attention and purely platonic social companionship*** for women. Not only in regard to women who I was interacting with in my personal life, but after that conversation with Anthony, even with female co-workers and business colleagues.

I am not the biggest fan of the term "game" unless I am referring to ***manipulative head games***, but I will go ahead and use this informal term as it relates to many men's attempts to connect with women romantically or strictly sexually.

If you are single heterosexual man who has been familiar with what is known as ***The Attraction & Seduction Industry***, or more informally, ***The Pickup Artist** (PUA) **Community***, you will hear the term 'game' used quite frequently.

The top two general types of *game with women* are ***verbal game*** and ***non-verbal game***.

Three examples of *non-verbal game* would be "**looks**" game *(i.e., when a man uses the aesthetic appeal of his facial looks and/or the visual appeal of his lean, muscular, athletic physique to motivate women to share his company sexually)*; "**masculine energy**" game or "**subcommunication**" game *(i.e., when a man uses non-verbal cues such as his eye contact, the manner in which he caresses and touches a woman's body, and his overall masculine demeanor and disposition in order to communicate his sexual desires and interest to a woman without going as far as to specifically verbalize his sexual desires and interests to her)*; and "**money, fame, and status**" game *(i.e., when a man relies on his degree of career success, financial success, and overall sense of fame, social status, and/or social* *popularity in order to enhance his chances of attracting beautiful and sexy women).*

As I mentioned already in the Introduction Chapter, there are two general types of *verbal game*: **direct** *(verbal)* **game** and **indirect** *(verbal)* **game**. My ***Mode One Approach*** is representative of **direct** (verbal) game. ***Mode Two*** Behavior and ***Mode Three*** Behavior is representative of **indirect** (verbal) game.

When I evaluate a man's verbal communication style, here are some factors I consider:

Does the man verbally communicate his desires, interests, and intentions to women in a manner that is **honest** or **dishonest**?

Does the man verbally communicate his desires, interests, and intentions to women in a manner that is **confident** or **non-confident**?

Does the man verbally communicate his desires, interests, and intentions to women in a manner that is **Alpha (strong and assertive)** or **Beta (weak and passive)**?

Does the man verbally communicate his desires, interests, and intentions to women in a manner that is **genuine, sincere, and serious** or **disingenuous, misleading, and/or lighthearted and facetious**?

Does the man verbally communicate his desires, interests, and intentions to women in a manner that is **very specific** or very **vague and ambiguous** and **beat-around-the-bush**?

Does the man verbally communicate his desires, interests, and intentions to women in a manner that is **provocative, or even profane and sexually explicit** or **conventional, polite, and cautious**?

Does the man verbally communicate his desires, interests, and intentions to women in a manner that is **charming, smooth, and seductive** or **awkward, angry, antagonistic, nervous, or 'creepy'**?

For example, many conventional PUAs will tell men that they essentially HAVE TO engage in 20 minutes, 30 minutes, 45 minutes, or an hour or more worth of entertaining small talk in order to make a woman feel more 'comfortable' in his presence. Instead of referring to this as *small talk*, *chit chat*, or *fluff talk*, they usually refer to this as "rapport building" or "building trust" conversation.

I don't agree with that concept. I believe in verbally communicating my romantic or strictly sexual desires, interests, and intentions to women within the first five minutes or less of my very first conversation with a woman. Again, this is the primary basis for my ***Mode One Approach*** and verbally bold and direct communication style.

Not only would I say that making a woman smile, giggle, or laugh has very little if anything to do with getting her sexually aroused, I would take it a step further and suggest that sometimes, your sense of humor can actually **prevent you** from motivating women to agree to engage in sexual relations with you. Don't believe me?

If there is one story from my past that I have shared with men dozens of times when I have been a featured speaker at various workshops as well as on a number of my YouTube-based video podcasts, is the story about when I was working for a health and fitness club in spring and summer 2000 while residing in Los Angeles.

One evening in summer 2000, I met these two very attractive Caucasian women who were working out in the club, and they let me know that their main objective was to develop a "rounder, more curvy butt" similar to what they felt most Black women possessed. They literally said, *"We want a butt like Black women have!"*

Later, both of them began lightheartedly flirting with me, so I began talking to them in a very X-rated, sexually explicit manner *(what I refer to in my other books as a* ***Mode One-HARDCORE*** *Approach)*. I went on to verbally communicate to them that I wanted to engage in a *ménage à trois* (i.e., a sexual threesome) with them. After a few minutes of mild resistance, they both agreed. They said, *"We love to be experimental ... so what the hell. Why not!"*

If I would have ended the conversation at that point on that Thursday evening, 99% chance, I would have been in bed with both of them on that subsequent Saturday evening. Instead, I ended up making a **huge tactical mistake** involving too much *small talk* and too heavy of a dose of *my comedic humor*.

Approximately ten minutes after our conversation inside the fitness club ended, I happened to notice that both of the women were standing outside on the sidewalk just East of Fairfax Avenue and Wilshire Boulevard intersection, across from The La Brea Tar Pits and Museum. At first, I thought they might have been waiting for the bus, but they remained on the sidewalk for at least twenty minutes while a number of buses passed them by.

So, for whatever reason, I chose to go outside to see if they were okay. Within a few minutes, I began engaging in a high degree of *fluff talk* with them, and then soon, I transitioned into "Alan, the former standup comedian" mode, and I began sharing jokes and humorous stories with the two young women.

On the positive end, I had them laughing *hysterically*. I mean, I literally had both women howling with laughter to the point where they were bending over and holding their stomachs from laughing so hard.

On the negative end, as I began to wrap up the conversation with them for the second time that evening, I reiterated that I looked forward to engaging in a sexual threesome with them in a couple of days. Sadly, this time, their attitude changed from earlier in the evening.

This time, the two women were like, *"Well, to be honest ... we don't really want you to come to our place for sex any longer ... we would rather you come over to our place to entertain us and make us laugh!!!"*

My facial expression went from lighthearted to irritated in a matter of seconds. I said, "Surely, you are joking …" and they responded, *"No! We are serious! We really want you to make us laugh!! We don't really want to have sex with you anymore. We would much prefer you come to our place to entertain us and make us laugh. You are extremely funny!!!"*

I cannot share with you how ticked off I was when I went back inside the health & fitness club. I mean, I was **seething**. Realistically though, I could not blame anyone one but myself.

Number one, I should have never gone outside to check on them. It made me look like I cared too much about their well-being *(something you should never do with women you're just interested in engaging in a one-night stand or a weekend fling with. Trust me on this)*.

Number two, once they informed me that they were just waiting for their cousin to pick them up, I should have immediately ended the conversation and went back inside the fitness club instead of performing 15-20 minutes' worth of impromptu 'street comedy' with them.

I was telling a client of mine not too long ago, that this story is not my only incident of this.

Beginning with my Freshman year in college at Indiana University, I have probably experienced at least a half dozen instances where a woman initially seemed to be very interested in engaging in sexual relations with me up until the point where I made the mistake of spending too much time in "standup comedian" mode. Next thing I knew, the women involved would let me know that they were no longer interested in engaging in sex with me.

This is what I have realized about the vast majority of women. Women love a great sense of humor in a man who is their husband, their fiancée, their long-term boyfriend, or their purely platonic friend or professional colleague. If you fall into one of those categories, showing women your 'funny' side repeatedly will not hurt you too much.

On the other hand, when it comes to being a woman's "fuck buddy" *(i.e., short-term casual sex lover)*, women generally prefer to hook up with a man who is more serious, more smooth and seductive, more laid back, and in some cases, even very intense, a bit 'edgy' and even seemingly "dangerous" *(the latter is why many women get turned on my criminal types and gangbanger types)*.

Even Eddie Murphy, the popular comedian and movie star, discussed this issue once. I was reading an interview he had years ago, and he offered this advice to another popular male entertainer (slightly paraphrased): *"Never try to be sexy, and hysterically funny, at the same time. You can be both sexy and hysterically funny in general, but never at the exact same moment in time."*

Based on my many experiences with women, I would generally agree with Murphy's assessment.

In the same way you have many women that will use and exploit men for flattery or for their financial & materialistic generosity, you have a number of women that will simply *use you* for your sense of humor and your willingness to entertain them when they are bored and/or lonely.

To reiterate, a *Manipulative Timewaster* is a woman that will mislead a man into believing that if he continues to behave in a manner that is pleasing to her, and he continues to perform financial and non-financial favors for her, that she will ultimately 'reward' him with one or more opportunities to engage in sexual relations with her … even though she knows deep down that she will **NEVER, EVER** allow that man to engage in sexual relations with her.

A man who is not afraid of being rejected by a woman will have no problem verbally communicating his romantic or strictly sexual desires, interests, and intentions to a woman in a ***Mode One*** manner. This type of man will usually be able to quickly identify and effectively weed out women who are *Manipulative Timewaster* types within the first ten-to-fifteen minutes of their very first conversation with a woman.

Many men foolishly believe that if they regularly or semi-regularly engage in trivial *chit chat*, *fluff talk*, and *small talk* with women, and generally operate as a woman's *Personal (Comedic) Entertainer*, they are going to earn some sort of valuable "Brownie Points" that they will be able to cash in at a later date for an opportunity to engage in sexual relations with a woman.

Any woman who is a *Manipulative Timewaster* type that specifically seeks out men to become her *Personal (Comedic) Entertainer* for a period of hours, days, weeks, months, or even years is generally known in society as an *Innocent Flirt*.

As I always tell men, it is okay to be 'casually witty' with women, but you should generally hold back on being intentionally and outright funny with women (particularly if your interest is **casual sex**).

I have known many women in my life that regularly maintained at least a dozen or more men in their social circle just to operate as *Personal (Comedic) Entertainers* for them.

Once a woman has you tabbed as a *Personal (Comedic) Entertainer*, there is a 99% chance that you are never, ever going to end up engaging in sexual relations with that woman. Why would any woman feel motivated to allow you to have sex with her, when she can experience lengthy and highly entertaining conversations with you **FOR FREE**.

If you are a man who falls into this category in your social interactions with women, I know for a fact that you have returned home after a number of social events feeling agitated, irritated, regretful, and sometimes just downright angry and frustrated.

Bottom line quit trying to be "Mr. Funny Man" around women all the time. Deep down, you are trying to perform as "Mr. Funny Man" in order to prevent yourself from being rejected, ignored, criticized, and/or insulted by women.

From this day forward, concentrate on being 'casually witty' instead of outright funny. Even more importantly, concentrate on verbally communicating your romantic or strictly sexual desires, interests, and intentions to women without all the lengthy and trivial *chit chat*, *fluff talk*, and *small talk*. Soon, you will notice that women will treat you with a higher degree of **Alpha male respect**. Trust me on this.

In the very next chapter, I am going to discuss men who regularly offer women **free meals**, **monetary favors**, and **materialistic gifts** in the hopes of motivating those women to engage in sexual relations with them.

Continue reading my friend.

## Men Who Offer Women Free Meals, Monetary Favors, and Materialistic Gifts in order to Win Favor with Them

The third of the **5 types of men** who I am going to discuss who go out of their way to prevent and avoid being rejected by women and hopefully prevent and avoid any and all forms of 'negative' reactions and responses from women are men who resort to offering women free meals, monetary favors, and/or materialistic gifts in the hopes of motivating women to engage in sexual relations with them. I generally refer to these types of men in my books as ***Mode Three 'Targets'*** ... but other men and women in society many times refer to these types of men as *chumps* or *simps*.

What is the difference between a man who operates as a *Trick* or *Sugar Daddy*, and a man who is categorized as a *simp* or *Mode Three 'Target'*?

A man who operates as a *Trick* is a man who offers financial compensation to a woman – usually, a **street prostitute**, **professional Call Girl**, or **upscale Erotic Escort** – directly for what appears to be *guaranteed* sexual companionship for him.

An example of *trickin'* would be if you contacted a professional Call Girl, and you offered to pay her $75.00 (USD) in exchange for her performing oral sex on you. The main problem with *trickin'* is that it is illegal in many cities and countries, due to the fact that in legal terms, *trickin'* is synonymous with "soliciting a woman for sex" (or even more formally, **solicitation of prostitution**), which is against the law in many geographical locations.

Similar to being a trick, is the idea of being a woman's *Sugar Daddy* or *Financial Sponsor*. When you are *Sugar Daddy* or *Financial Sponsor* for a woman, you never offer women money **directly** in exchange for their sexual companionship. What you do instead is offer to pay for many of women's social activities and/or month-to-month living expenses, and you and the woman maintain an unwritten agreement that she will 'reward' your financial generosity with access to her sexual companionship either regularly, semi-regularly, or occasionally. This type of behavior is generally known as *Wining & Dining* a woman.

With a man who is a *chump or a simp*, the biggest thing that separates him from the *Trick* or the *Sugar Daddy* is that the *chump* or *simp* **never, ever verbalizes his desire to have sex with the woman of interest at all**. The *simp* or *Mode Three 'Target'* type just assumes that the woman of interest somehow knows that he strongly desires to engage in sex with her *(which in reality, is usually true)*.

Consequently, the man who is the *chump* or *simp* ends up spending a significant amount of money on women only to end up sharing their company in a **non-physical, non-sexual, purely platonic manner** with the long-standing *hope* that the woman will one day soon just happen to grant him permission to engage in sexual relations with her.

Remember, in the very last chapter, I discussed the concept of *verbal game vs. non-verbal game*, and I mentioned how one form of non-verbal game is known as "**masculine energy**" and/or "**subcommunication**."

Ever since the early-to-mid 2000s, if not a bit earlier, I have always had a number of male critics of mine offer comments to me along the lines of, *"Alan, I don't believe you should ever straightforwardly verbalize your sexual desires, interests, and intentions to women. Ever. I believe you should simply **imply** your interest in having sex with a woman with various forms of **sexual innuendo** and **subcommunication**. If you go as far as to straightforwardly verbalize your sexual desires and interests directly to a woman, you're pretty much asking to be rejected."*

I have always maintained this belief: if you agree with that sort of assessment, then plain and simple, you are a man who has never, ever socially interacted with a woman who is seasoned, savvy, highly materialistic *Manipulative Timewaster* type.

You see, the primary factor that allows women who are *Manipulative Timewasters* to exploit and take advantage of *Mode Three 'Target' types* is **just that**. A man cannot rely exclusively on non-verbal forms of communication with women when he is dealing with a woman who is an *Attention Whore* type, a *Cock-Teaser* type, a *Financial Favor Seeker* type, or a *Manipulative Timewaster* type in general.

This warning and assessment are not simply representative of just my own personal opinion. Women who have operated for years as *Manipulative Timewaster* types with dozens and hundreds of men have literally shared this insight with me on multiple occasions if those women happened to be close friends or friendly acquaintances of mine.

Anytime a man attempts to *hide*, *deny*, *camouflage*, and/or *suppress* his true sexual desires, interests, and intentions from women, **he automatically opens the door** for a *Manipulative Timewaster* to **'run game'** on him. Guaranteed.

As I have pointed out a number of times over the last twenty-plus years, there are really only three types of sexual interest a woman ever maintains toward a man:

- **Genuine sexual interest** *(otherwise known as **lust**)*
- **Manipulative & Opportunistic sexual interest** *(the type of sexual interest that a woman who operates as a street prostitute, professional Call Girl, upscale Erotic Escort, Sugar Baby or general Gold Digger type would maintain with men they socialize with)*
- **Coerced and/or Non-Consensual sexual interest** *(if a woman only agrees to have sex with a man because she has drugs and/or alcohol in her system, or she feels physically threatened, or at minimum, she has been misled and emotionally manipulated by a man to believe that he genuinely loves her and is interested in maintaining a long-term romantic relationship with her, this would represent coerced and/or non-consensual sexual interest)*

The 4th type of sexual interest would simply be **no sexual interest** at all.

A man who is a *chump*, *simp*, *Mode Three 'Target'* type, *Trick*, or *Sugar Daddy / Financial Sponsor* will never, ever experience genuine sexual interest *(i.e., lust)*. Ever.

In best case scenario, a man who operates as a *Trick* and/or a *Sugar Daddy / Financial Sponsor* might experience some form of *manipulative & opportunistic type sex* with women, but that is only if they develop the confidence and courage to verbally communicate their true sexual desires, interests, and intentions to women in an upfront and straightforwardly honest manner *(in other words, they have the Balls & Backbone to be* ***Mode One*** *with women)*.

In worst case scenario, men who exhibit the behavior of a *chump, simp,* or *Mode Three 'Target' type* for too long might become extremely angry, irritated, and sexually frustrated to the point where they will resort to some sort of sexual assault *(such as rape or date-rape)*, or at minimum, they will resort to operating as a **blatant liar who is willing to psychologically and emotionally manipulate women** in an attempt to get in their pants.

I rarely if ever have offered women free meals, monetary favors, and/or materialistic gifts in direct exchange for their sexual companionship. For example, I never offer to treat a woman to a free meal on a lunch date or dinner date if I know ahead of time that my only interest is one or more episodes of short-term, non-monogamous 'casual' sex. Beginning with the age of 22, the only women I have ever invited on a lunch date and/or dinner date were women who I viewed as a potential long-term girlfriend or future wife. The last time I resorted to *trickin'* with women was when I visited Amsterdam's infamous *Red-Light District* in late 2010.

There is another fairly popular dating coach who wrote in his book that if a man is perceived by women as being average looking or less-than-average looking, then he pretty much HAS TO take a woman out on two or three dates in order to gain any chance of engaging in sexual relations with that woman.

This dating coach went on to explain in his book that he believes that men who were not blessed with God-given good looks and/or a silver-tongued smooth and seductive *mouthpiece* can only gain the chance at possibly "increasing" a woman's (sexual) interest by offering her free meals and displaying his great sense of humor and other appealing aspects of his personality during the lunch date or dinner date.

It is obvious that this other dating coach does not understand the three different types of sexual interest that I already described in this chapter.

Realistic fact: a man cannot "purchase" **GENUINE SEXUAL INTEREST** (lust) from a woman via free meals, monetary favors, offers of employment or job promotions, or expensive materialistic gifts. It is literally **impossible**. A man would be wasting his time even attempting to do such a thing.

The only type of sexual interest you will receive from a woman when you offer her various things of **tangible value** is what I already described as *Manipulative & Opportunistic* sexual interest. In other words, the only reason this woman is allowing you to engage in sexual relations with her is because you are offering her something of monetary or materialistic value.

Another realistic fact: You cannot 'create' or 'increase' **GENUINE** sexual interest (lust). Genuine sexual interest is either there, or not there. Inviting a woman to join you on three lunch dates or dinner dates is not going to help you 'increase' or 'enhance' a woman's lust for you. Lust is either present in a woman, or it is not present.

Now, if you own my book ***Oooooh … Say it Again***, you already know that many women will indeed attempt to hide, deny, camouflage, or suppress their lust for a man *(usually because of their fear of being 'slut-shamed')*. This is what women who are *Wholesome Pretenders* and *Erotic Hypocrites* do.

You see, there is a difference between **Attraction**, **Seduction**, **Dishonesty & Manipulation**, **Financial Negotiation**, and **Coercion**. Here is a brief explanation of each:

**ATTRACTION**: In real simple terms, this is when you meet a woman who not only possesses a high degree of genuine sexual interest (lust) toward you, but she is not afraid to straightforwardly let you know that she is very interested in engaging sexual relations with you. With a woman like this (what I refer to in my books as a *Reciprocator*), you would not need to offer this woman any free meals, monetary favors, or materialistic gifts … and to take it step further, you would not even necessarily have to possess a very charming and persuasive *mouthpiece*. Just about all of her attraction centers on a man's **physical appearance** and his degree of **masculine sex appeal**.

**SEDUCTION**: When a woman is a *Reciprocator*, she does not need to be *persuaded* or *seduced* into engaging in sexual relations with a man. On the other hand, when a woman is a *Wholesome Pretender* or an *Erotic Hypocrite*, she most certainly needs to be charmed, persuaded, and seduced into engaging in sexual relations with a man, and especially if that man is proposing some form of **short-term** and/or **non-monogamous** sex.

Even if a woman finds you physically attractive and sexually appealing, she is going to be reluctant to openly acknowledge an interest in short-term and/or non-monogamous 'casual' sex with a man for fear that it might have a negative effect on her public image and social reputation at some point in the near or distant future. In order to seduce women, you must develop a personality and a set of verbal communication skills that are **confident**, **charming**, **charismatic**, and extremely **persuasive**. When a man's manner of verbal expression with women is very *smooth* and *seductive*, this is what is known as a man possessing a *mouthpiece*. To put it another way, when you possess a smooth and seductive *mouthpiece,* this simply means that you have very strong ***verbal game*** with women.

**<u>DISHONESTY & MANIPULATION</u>**: Go back and reference my three types of sexual interest. The third type of sexual interest I highlighted is "**Coerced and/or Non-Consensual sexual interest**." If a man resorts to blatant dishonesty as well as disingenuous and misleading behavior with women in an attempt to manipulate them to agree to engage in sexual relations with him, then he would be employing ***emotional fraud*** with women.

A common example of this would be a man giving a woman the very misleading impression that he is interested in entering into a long-term, emotionally profound, strictly monogamous romantic relationship with her … when in reality, he just wants to enjoy one or more episodes of short-term non-monogamous 'casual' sex with her. If that woman has sex with that man, she is not truly consenting to engage in casual sex with him. She is consenting to engage in long-term relationship sex with him. Believe it or not, there are many women who view this type of deception by men as borderline **date-rape**. I am not sure if I would agree that lying to a woman and/or psychologically and emotionally manipulating a woman should be viewed as a punishable **crime**, but I definitely agree that such behavior is **highly unethical** and **I very much frown** on such behavior.

**FINANCIAL NEGOTIATION**: As I have already emphasized earlier in this chapter, anytime you are offering a woman money, financial favors, offers of employment, job or career promotions, free meals, free movie tickets, free concert tickets, expensive materialistic gifts, and anything else of tangible and monetary or materialistic value, then you are intentionally (or unintentionally) engaging in a form of **financial negotiation** for sex. Again, the two main forms of financial negotiation are *trickin'* and *Wining & Dining*. *Trickin'* is the most **verbally direct** form of financial negotiation for sex, but it is also the most legally risky depending on what city, county, state, or country you reside in. *Wining & Dining* can be verbally communicated in a very direct manner, or a man's sexual desires and interests can be verbally communicated to a woman in a manner that is a bit more **indirect** and **vague & ambiguous**. Either way, at least a man eventually allows his sexual desires and interests to be known to a woman, and he fully understands that her sexual interest in him will be more along the lines of *Manipulative & Opportunistic* rather than *Genuine and Lustful*. Unlike *trickin'* and *Wining & Dining*, when a man is a *chump, simp* or *Mode Three 'Target' type*, he neither directly or indirectly verbally communicates his sexual desires and interests to women. The man simply offers to spend money on women regularly or semi-regularly with the hopeful wish and assumption that she is going to eventually decide to magically have sex with him.

**COERCION**: This method of attempting to get women to agree to engage in sex with a man is the most unacceptable and despicable. I will go into more detail about this category in **Chapter Five**. Anytime you attempt to impose yourself on a woman physically, and essentially attempt to ***force her*** to agree to engage in sex with you, then you are guilty of ***coercion***. A less physical means of coercion would be allowing a woman to consume a high degree of alcoholic beverages and/or (illegal) drugs, and then you seek to undermine and compromise her ability to offer you full, enthusiastic consent with a sober mind and objective intelligence. Men usually resort to this alternative when they feel as though attraction methods have failed them, seduction methods have failed them, dishonesty and manipulation methods have failed them, and their attempts at financial negotiation have been repeatedly rebuffed.

**Bottom line?** Don't ever make the mistake of confusing and conflating the concepts of *dishonesty & manipulation* and *financial negotiation* with **attraction** and/or **seduction**. They are not remotely the same thing.

Many women become **master manipulators** when they are in the company of men who they perceive as *chumps*, *simps*, or *Mode Three 'Targets.'* Don't be THAT guy.

Men who resort to **excessive flattery** of women foolishly believe that they will be able to provoke *genuine sexual interest* (lust) from women, when the reality is, they will end up as nothing more than a woman's personal *Ego Booster & Self-Esteem Booster*.

Men who resort to **engaging in lengthy and trivial, but highly entertaining small talk** with women foolishly believe that they will be able to provoke genuine sexual interest (lust) from women, when the reality is, they will end up as nothing more than a woman's *Personal (Comedic) Entertainer*.

Men who resort to **offering women free meals, monetary favors, and expensive materialistic gifts** foolishly believe that they will be able to provoke or increase a woman's sense of *genuine sexual interest* (lust), when the reality is, they will end up only provoking a woman's sense of ***manipulative & opportunistic*** sexual interest if they operate as a *Trick* or a *Sugar Daddy / Sponsor* … and even worse, they will end up being viewed by women as a *chump, simp, or Mode Three 'Target' type* which means they will **never** end up engaging in sexual relations with any woman they pursue.

In the very next chapter, I am going discuss at least one more disingenuous and misleading method that many men in society employ in an attempt to prevent or avoid abrupt, harsh, or straightforward rejections from women. I refer to this method as *FunClubbing*, which is essentially the **non-financial** equivalent to the concept of *simping*.

Continue reading my friend.

## Men Who Pretend to be Only Interested in Being a Woman's Platonic Friend in order to Win Favor with Them

The fourth of the **5 types of men** who I am going to discuss who go out of their way to prevent and avoid being rejected by women and hopefully prevent and avoid any and all forms of 'negative' reactions and responses from women are men who temporarily or indefinitely mislead women into believing that they are genuinely content with remaining that woman's purely platonic male 'friend,' when in reality, these men know deep down that they would prefer to engage in a series of social interactions with these women that are more romantic or strictly sexual.

The unique term I use to describe this type of behavior by men is *FunClubbing*. I first became familiar with this term back in November 1981 when I was a freshman in college at Indiana University in Bloomington, Indiana. A friend, future fraternity brother of mine, and former high school classmate of mine by the name of Charles Taliefero was the first man to use that term with me.

One afternoon, Charles and I were having lunch together in the cafeteria of our university's dormitory, and he looked a bit frustrated and irritated. So, I asked him, "Charlie … is everything okay with you?" At first, he said, *"I'm good. It's nothing,"* but then he maintained this facial expression of irritation. So, I asked him again, "Charlie, are you sure you're okay?" Finally, he opened up. Charles said to me, *"Alan, if you don't remember anything else I tell you as it relates to dealing with women, remember this: never allow yourself to become a member of a woman's 'Fun Club' ..."*

Of course, I had no idea what he meant by that advice and cautionary warning. So, I asked him to explain what he meant in more detail. Charles obliged.

Charles went on to explain that being in a woman's 'Fun Club' means that you are regularly spending time with a woman … at minimum, let's say an hour or two per day, many times more than that, sometimes a little less than that … and deep down, you really want that woman to become your next long-term girlfriend or next casual sex lover, but you just do not have the confidence or courage to let that woman know that in an upfront, straightforwardly honest, ***Mode One*** manner.

Consequently, all that time you end up spending with a woman ends up being for nothing. It never leads to you dating that woman in the near or distant future, and it never leads to you engaging in casual sex with that woman in the near or distant future. What happens is, a man ends up spending time with the woman of interest "just for fun," hence the term, her 'Fun Club.'

For the remainder of my years at Indiana University, that became a heavily used term among my fraternity brothers *(I have been a member of **Kappa Alpha Psi** fraternity since November 4, 1982)*. Anytime we recognized that a fraternity brother of ours was spending a significant amount of time with a woman, and the woman involved seemed to be under the impression that she and my fraternity brother were 'just friends only' and that they had been hanging out together 'just for fun' *(with no real potential of any sort of developing romance or sexual intimacy)* but all of us in the fraternity knew he wanted something more romantic or strictly sexual with the woman, we would lightheartedly warn the fraternity brother involved, "You are FunClubbing!!! Stop FunClubbing!!!"

I have been guilty of *FunClubbing* with at least a dozen women in my adult life. If there was one particular scenario that always led to me *FunClubbing* was when I met a woman who at the time I met her, was already romantically involved with some other man, or she was already engaging in casual sex with another man who I was friends with, but then later on, this same woman became single and available to be intimate with other men.

Anytime I hear a man expressing a comment such as, "Linda placed me in her friend zone, and never allowed me to come out," I always go out of my way to correct them. In reality, no woman can truly 'place you' in her just-friends-only zone. Only **YOU** can place yourself in a woman's just-friends-only zone. *FunClubbing* is usually Step #1 in this process.

In real simple terms, *FunClubbing* is to investing **time** into pursuing a woman's romantic or strictly sexual companionship what *simping* is to investing **money** and **offering women financial favors, free meals, and expensive materialistic gifts** in an attempt to hopefully one day gain the opportunity to spend time with that woman romantically or for one or more episodes of short-term non-monogamous casual sex. Both forms of behavior will rarely if ever lead to you engaging in either relationship sex or casual sex with a woman.

The weakness with both forms of behavior by men is a combination of their severe lack of confidence and courage *(i.e., Balls)*, their ineffective verbal communication skills and overall social skills, and **their profound fear of being rejected and/or**

**being indefinitely ignored** by a woman that they are very attracted to.

All women love to gain some degree of access to a man's **non-sexual** time, attention, and companionship for **FREE** *(i.e., without feeling obligated to engage in sexual relations with the man)*, and especially women who operate as *Manipulative Timewasters*.

Now let me reiterate this: If a woman expresses to you from your very first social interaction with her that all she is interested in is nothing more than a purely platonic friendship with you, then you cannot validly categorize that woman as a *Manipulative Timewaster* at some point in the future. In that scenario, the woman gave you a heads up that you have virtually a zero percent chance of engaging in sexual relations with her at any time in the near or distant future.

A true *Manipulative Timewaster* type would never come straight out and say, "I have no interest in having sex with you." That is something a *Rejecter* would do. A *Manipulative Timewaster* would go out of her way to verbally communicate her interests (or lack thereof) in a very **vague and ambiguous** manner.

In other words, a woman who operates as a *Manipulative Timewaster* would never make an effort to straightforwardly **reciprocate** a man's sexual desires and interests … but at the same time, she would never go as far as to straightforwardly **reject** a man's sexual desires and interests either. To do either would undermine her own ability to *run game* on a man and manipulate him for her self-serving objectives.

There are at least two situations where a man will never, ever have to worry about being taken advantage of by a woman who operates as a *Manipulative Timewaster*:

1) When a man always verbally communicates his romantic or strictly sexual desires, interests, and intentions to a woman in a confident, highly self-assured, upfront, specific, and straightforwardly honest manner; In other words, he always exhibits ***Mode One*** behavior with women; A *Mode One* verbal communication style prevents women from remaining in what I refer to as "**The Vague & Ambiguous Zone,**" which in turn, prevents women from engaging in *manipulative 'head games'* with him;

2) The second situation that will prevent many men from being taken advantage of by women who operate as *Manipulative Timewasters* are men who perceived by women as being either **a)** broke and/or cheap or **b)** boring or 'weird & creepy.'

In relation to situation #2, you have to always remember that women who operate as *Manipulative Timewasters* always want to exploit men for one of these two things if not both: 1) **your sense of financial and materialistic generosity** and/or 2) **your flattering, entertaining, and emotionally empathetic personality and non-physical, non-sexual social companionship**.

If a woman feels that she cannot exploit you for either one of those two self-serving benefits, then she is not going to waste time attempting to mislead you and manipulate you.

One thing I have found from my experiences and observations is that most women are reluctant to engage in frequent episodes of casual sex with men unless they have one or more men in their life who provide them with financial and non-financial 'favors' … and … one or more men in their life who provide them with flattering, entertaining, and emotionally empathetic non-physical and non-sexual social companionship.

Put another way, many women will not reveal and unleash the most kinky and promiscuous aspect of their personality and sexual behavior until they have secured at least one man in their life who fulfills their **non-sexual** wants and needs.

This could be their husband, their fiancé, their long-term boyfriend, or one or more of their purely platonic male friends. As much as women desire men's sexual attention and companionship, they generally desire and value a man's **non-sexual** time, attention, and companionship **even more**.

Blunt truth? Hypothetically, if you eliminated all women's desire for financial and non-financial 'favors' from men, and you eliminated all women's desire for flattering, entertaining, and emotionally empathetic non-physical and non-sexual attention and social companionship from men, there would be a LARGE PERCENTAGE of men in society that would be **completely and indefinitely ignored by women**. REAL TALK. Some men would never gain the opportunity to share a woman's company without explicitly paying for it.

A lot of men in *The Manosphere* foolishly believe that if they are too candid and forthright with women about their true sexual desires, interests, and intentions *(i.e., Mode One),* it will place them in a disadvantageous and vulnerable position with women, which would consequently make it easier for women to exploit them and manipulate them.

Nothing could be further from the truth.

If anything, the truth of the situation is that it is literally **just the opposite**. Upfront, straightforward honesty does **not** place a man in a vulnerable position to be easily manipulated by a woman. It is when a man presents himself as **impatient and desperate** for a woman's romantic or strictly sexual companionship ... or when a man's verbal communication style is **vague and ambiguous** (and **dishonest**, **disingenuous**, and **misleading**) ... that he will find himself in a position where many women can easily mislead and manipulate him.

I have been exhibiting ***Mode One*** behavior with women since August 1984, and I have never experienced a *Manipulative Timewaster* type being in a position where she could potentially mislead me and/or manipulate me after I verbally communicated to that woman straightforwardly that I was interested in exchanging orgasms with her.

Upfront, straightforward honesty **neutralizes** the *manipulative 'head games'* of women who operate as *Manipulative Timewasters*. Again, even women who I have known personally who admitted to being a *Manipulative Timewaster* type with multiple men have repeatedly confessed this to me over the years. ***Mode One*** behavior always allows men to quickly identify and effectively weed out women who operate as *Manipulative Timewaster* types.

Everything begins with your **fear of being rejected and indefinitely ignored by women** … and secondly, your **fear of being harshly criticized, insulted, and/or disliked by women**.

Anytime a man indefinitely maintains those two fears while socially interacting with women, his behavior and verbal communication style is going to become . . .

- Cowardly
- Dishonest to one degree or another
- Disingenuous and Misleading
- Duplicitous and Highly Manipulative
- Vague and Ambiguous

A man who regularly exhibits ***Mode One*** behavior with women is a man who has overcome his profound fear of being rejected or indefinitely ignored by a woman whom he finds physically attractive and sexually appealing.

A man who regularly exhibits ***Mode One*** behavior with women is a man who has overcome his profound fear of being harshly criticized, insulted, and/or disliked by a woman whom he finds physically attractive and sexually appealing.

It is the fear of being rejected and indefinitely ignored that directly motivates men to exhibit some variation of ***Mode Three*** behavior with women, and it is the fear of being harshly criticized, insulted, and/or disliked by women that directly motivates men to exhibit some variation of ***Mode Two*** behavior with women.

Let's say by some chance, you have frequently exhibited some variation of *Mode Two* behavior with women and/or *Mode Three* behavior with women … and you feel totally satisfied with both the **quality** of your (long-term and short-term) sex partners as well as the **quantity** of your (long-term and short-term) sex partners … then more power to you. You will probably never gain the motivation to transition to a ***Mode One*** verbal communication style with women. You will remain as you are today.

Realistically though, no man is going to experience a high degree of long-lasting success with women when he regularly exhibits some variation of ***Mode Three*** behavior with women because such behavior is representative of being a blatant liar, a disingenuous and misleading manipulator of women's emotions, a cheater or an adulterer, or if nothing else, a long-standing **verbal coward**.

To a slightly lesser extent, even many men who choose to exhibit some variation of ***Mode Two*** behavior with women are going to find themselves feeling disappointed and unsatisfied as well as feeling disingenuous and duplicitous after their many social interactions with women and just generally a wee bit frustrated with their love life, sex life, and overall social life.

Many men who become frustrated with their ineffective attempts to get laid with women by excessively flattering women (Chapter One), entertaining women (Chapter Two), *simping* with women (Chapter Three), and *FunClubbing* with women (this chapter) might find themselves eventually resorting to more desperate and aggressive *(not to mention, unethical and illegal)* means of preventing women from rebuffing their sexual desires and interests. This could include groping women, raping or date-raping women, or some other form of sexual harassment and sexual assault.

I will discuss the men who fall into this category in the very next chapter, Chapter Five.

Continue reading my friend.

## Men Who Seek to Circumvent and/or Compromise Women's Ability to Provide Them with Verbal (Sexual) Consent

The fifth of the **5 types of men** who I am going to discuss who go out of their way to prevent and avoid being rejected by women and hopefully prevent and avoid having their sexual advances abruptly rebuffed by women is going to be different than the first four types of men that I have discussed in Chapter One, Chapter Two, Chapter Three, and Chapter Four.

In the first four chapters, I focused on men who resort to **flattering women excessively** in an attempt to prevent and avoid rejection (Chapter One); men who resort to **engaging in lengthy and trivial, but highly entertaining and emotionally empathetic *chit chat*, *fluff talk*, and *small talk* with women** in an attempt to prevent and avoid rejection (Chapter Two); men who resort to **offering women free meals, free movie tickets, free concert tickets, other assorted monetary favors, and expensive materialistic gifts** in an attempt to prevent and avoid rejection (Chapter Three); and finally, men who resort to **giving women the very disingenuous and misleading impression that they are content with**

**maintaining a non-physical, non-sexual, purely platonic 'friendship' with them indefinitely** in an attempt to prevent and avoid both being rejected as well as being indefinitely ignored by women of interest (Chapter Four).

Other than attempting to prevent and avoid being rejected by women, the second main common denominator among these four groups of men is that they place themselves in a position where they can be easily taken advantage of by women who operate as what I refer to as a *Manipulative Timewaster*.

Once again, a *Manipulative Timewaster* represents any woman who seeks to either **a)** gain temporary or indefinite access to a man's **non-sexual** time, attention, and companionship without ever agreeing to allow that man to engage in sexual relations with her and/or **b)** gain temporary or indefinite access to a man's financial and materialistic generosity without ever going as far as to allow the male target to engage in sexual relations with her.

This type of woman is exceptionally good at giving naïve and horny men the very disingenuous and extremely misleading impression that they have at least a CHANCE at gaining the opportunity to engage in sexual relations with the woman at some point in the near and/or distant future, when in reality, these women know for a fact that they will never allow these men to engage in sexual relations with them.

This manipulative tactic used by women was the basis for the original title of this book, ***The Possibility of Sex: How Naïve and Lustful Men are Manipulated by Women Regularly***, which again, I published as an eBook in October 2012 and as an audiobook in November 2014.

The group of men I am about to describe in this chapter are a bit different. The men I will be describing in this chapter are not at all seeking to 'win the favor' of women or earn 'brownie points' from women that they might be able to 'cash in' later in exchange for a woman's short-term or long-term sexual companionship. No, not at all.

The men I will be describing in this chapter have moved past the point of attempting to win over women with flattery, entertaining and emotionally empathetic small talk, free meals, monetary favors and materialistic gifts, and/or a prolonged 'fake friendship.'

Forget that. These men have already attempted using flattery and insincere compliments as a means of trying to get in a woman's pants, and those attempts failed.

These men have already attempted engaging in highly entertaining, emotionally empathetic and trivial small talk with women as a means of trying to get in a woman's pants, and those attempts failed.

These men have already attempted to offer women free meals, free movie tickets, free concert tickets, monetary favors, and materialistic gifts, but they still ended up in a woman's dreaded 'just-friends-only' category.

These men have already attempted to hide, deny, camouflage, and suppress their true romantic and/or strictly sexual desires, interests, and intentions temporarily or indefinitely under the disingenuous and misleading guise of maintaining a 'purely platonic friendship' with women … but in the end, this weak tactic left them feeling incredibly bitter and frustrated toward women.

The men I will be describing in this chapter have already attempted using ***Mode Two*** behavior with women *(i.e., behavior that is vague and ambiguous, and manipulative in a very subtle manner)* and in some cases, they have already executed a couple of specific variations of ***Mode Three*** behavior *(i.e., behavior that is cowardly, blatantly dishonest, disingenuous and misleading, and psychologically, emotionally, and financially manipulative)*. So, here they are.

Right now, I want you to reference everything I discussed beginning on **page 51** and ending on **page 59**. In that latter portion of Chapter Three, I highlighted the fact that there are only **three (3) types of sexual interest a woman can have for a man**.

Again, those three types of interest would be:

a) **Genuine sexual interest**, otherwise known simply as *lust*;

b) **Manipulative & Opportunistic sexual interest**, which would represent when a woman only agrees to engage in sexual relations with a man after the man has offered her money, financial favors, an offer of employment or job promotion, some expensive materialistic gifts, and other items of tangible value in exchange for her (short-term or long-term) sexual companionship;

c) **Coerced and/or Non-Consensual sexual interest**, which would represent when a woman only agrees to engage in sexual relations with a man because a man has **a)** led her to believe that he is genuinely in love with her and has a strong desire to maintain a long-term, emotionally profound, strictly monogamous romantic relationship with her;

**b)** has provoked her to consume drugs and/or alcoholic beverages so that she can no longer provide verbal (sexual) consent to him in a sober state of mine; or **c)** threatened her with physical harm, torture, or murder.

Every type of man that will be discussed in the remainder of this chapter will be the type of man that only receives *Coerced and/or Non-Consensual sexual interest* from women. I will begin with men who are **blatant liars** and **psychological and emotional manipulators of women**.

## BLATANT LIARS and MANIPULATORS

If a single heterosexual man cannot seem to experience romantic or casual sex success with women as a result of **physical attraction** *(i.e., using the aesthetic appeal of his face, physique, and masculine demeanor and disposition)* and/or **verbal seduction** *(i.e., using the auditory appeal of his voice, his conversation skills, his erotic dirty talk talents, and his persuasive charm)*, then the first alternative he is going to resort to is some form of **disingenuous and vague & ambiguous behavior** *(i.e., pretty much everything I discussed in Chapter One, Chapter Two, and Chapter Four)*, or some form of **financial manipulation** *(i.e., pretty much everything I discussed in Chapter Three)*.

If the man finds that disingenuous and vague & ambiguous behavior and financial manipulation seems to be ineffective, then the very next alternative he is going to resort to is **blatantly dishonest** behavior and **psychological and emotional manipulation**.

Technically, even *FunClubbing* – which I discussed in Chapter Four – could fall into this category. When a man is FunClubbing with women, not only is he being *disingenuous* and *misleading*, but even more so, he is being completely *dishonest* with women. The only difference is, when a man is guilty of *FunClubbing*, he is usually **lying by omission** rather than **lying by commission**.

To refresh your memory on the difference between the two types of dishonesty, *lying by omission* is when you intentionally hold on to or suppress truthful information from someone. For example, if you were only interested in engaging in one or more episodes of short-term non-monogamous 'casual' sex with a woman of interest, but you allowed a number of hours, days, weeks, or months to pass by without you ever expressing those specific sexual desires and interests to the woman. This would represent you *lying by omission.*

Conversely, *lying by commission* is when you blatantly and intentionally express false and invalid information to someone. For example, if you were to verbally communicate to a woman that you were very interested in entering into a long-term, emotionally profound, strictly monogamous romantic relationship with her, even though you knew deep down that your only real interest was to engage in one or more episodes of short-term non-monogamous 'casual' sex with this same woman.

Just about all the men who I described in the first three chapters, and to a slightly lesser extent, Chapter Four, are men who have been guilty of *lying by omission*. If you are not just a liar, but a **blatant liar**, that automatically means that you are guilty of *lying by commission.*

For those of you reading this book who are very familiar with my backstory, you will remember that it was the issue of *blatant liars* and *psychological & emotional manipulators* that contributed to the initial development of my ***Mode One Approach*** philosophy back in 1984.

For those who may not be familiar with my full backstory, when I was a college student at Indiana University in the 1980s, I once had a conversation with three women who were members of *Alpha Kappa Alpha Sorority, Inc*. regarding men on campus (including a number of my own fraternity brothers) who were willing to lie to women and manipulate women psychologically and emotionally in order to gain opportunities to engage in short-term and/or non-monogamous sex with them.

Once in fall 1984, these three women asked me for my explanation of why men were willing to do such a thing with women. My response to the three women was, "Men who are willing to give women the misleading impression that they are open to entering into a long-term relationship with them are men who do not have the confidence or courage to let women know upfront and straightforwardly that they are only interested in a few episodes of (short-term non-monogamous) casual sex."

All three women just frowned. Then one of the three said, *"But WHY? Why are they so scared to straightforwardly tell us that all they want is (short-term non-monogamous) casual sex? I mean, REALLY? For all they know, that is all we might want too! I don't get it. I don't like all of these damn head games that men like to play with women."*

I will never forget what that same woman said to me after that last question and comment. First, her and her two sorority sisters gave each other this 'coded' facial expression, and then they all smirked at each other, Then, the same woman who asked me the last question said to me, *"Alan, I am going to be blunt honest with you. Us women?* ***We know the type of men that we want to engage in casual sex only with. We know. And those type of men are usually totally different than the type of men who we want as long-term boyfriends or husbands.*** *Just as I am sure that most of you men have different criteria for the women you want as your long-term companions versus the women you want to be with for only a one-night stand or weekend fling. In a nutshell, I don't want a man 'pretending' to be interested in being my long-term boyfriend when in reality, all he wants to do is 'hit it and quit it.' That shit is foul. I believe that every woman on this campus would agree that shit is foul."*

As most of my long-time followers and supporters know, **initially**, I lightheartedly referred to the three sorority sisters as naïve and opinionated "whiners and complainers."

Then, approximately two or three days later, I began to contemplate more on what the one woman said, and then **I began to side with her** and her two sorority sisters. After that, as they say, **the rest is history**. It was that conversation with those three AKA sorority sisters that heavily contributed to the formation of my *Mode One Approach* philosophy in fall of 1984 and for years and decades afterward.

Plain and simple, I don't care for men who are *blatant liars and seek to manipulate women psychologically and emotionally*. Like the one AKA said, I believe that shit is **FOUL**. I view men who are not upfront and straightforwardly honest with women about their desire for casual sex only as **verbal cowards**.

Sadly, as most men in *The Manosphere* already know, there are many pickup artists (PUAs) and dating coaches who actually FULLY ENDORSE and ENTHUSIASTICALLY PROMOTE the concept of lying to women and manipulating them psychologically and emotionally in an attempt to get in their pants. Personally, I will **never** go the "verbal coward" route to getting laid. I have too much moral character and integrity to stoop that low. I am all about "ethical womanizing."

Here's the thing: morals, values, and ethics aside, you can actually **get played** by a seasoned, savvy *Manipulative Timewaster* type by resorting to blatant dishonesty and psychological & emotional manipulation. **Trust me on this**. I know many men who were under the impression that they were successfully 'running game' on women, only to later realize in the long run that it was those women who were actually ***'running game' on THEM***.

If you read my original and later versions of my book, *Mode One*, you know that I highly emphasize this one real fact: **MANIPULATION IS ALWAYS POTENTIALLY A TWO-WAY STREET**.

In other words, the more dishonest you are with women … and the more attempts you put forth to manipulate women psychologically & emotionally … the more you actually OPEN YOURSELF UP to being the *victim* of women's own dishonesty and manipulative tactics. **A lot of men still don't fully realize this**.

Again, I have no respect for men who are blatant liars and psychological & emotional manipulators of women. The reality is, there have been some men who have actually been murdered because of toying with a woman's emotions.

Other men I know had their homes and other material possessions of theirs vandalized as a direct result of toying with the emotions of one or more women.

At bare minimum, I have known a number of men who had women become *obsessive stalkers* (think about the movies ***Play Misty for Me*** and ***Fatal Attraction***) because they were guilty of toying with the emotions of one or more women.

All I have to say is, if you're willing to resort to this sort of behavior, then be prepared to handle **all** of the potential consequences, repercussions, and acts of revenge and retribution that come along with it.

## MEN WHO DATE-RAPE WOMEN

When I attended college at Indiana University between August 1981 and August 1985, there was really no such thing as "Acquaintance Rape" or "Date-Rape." I did not first hear the term "date-rape" until the early-to-mid 1990s, and this was due in large part because of a woman who years later I had the opportunity to interview and collaborate with, and this woman's name is **Katie Koestner**.

Koestner was featured on the cover of *TIME Magazine* in June 1991 with the words "DATE RAPE" in big, bold letters. To this day, Ms. Koestner is considered one of the U.S.A.'s leading activists on sexual assault and date-rape prevention.

There are generally two forms of date-rape:

1) Date-rape involving the use of physical force
2) Date-rape involving the use of drugs and/or alcoholic beverages

Most incidents of date-rape usually involve BOTH **#1** (i.e., some degree of **physical force** on behalf of the man involved) and **#2** (i.e., some ingestion or consumption of **drugs and/or liquor**).

In my adult life, I actually prevented two incidents of date-rape. The first time was when I was a student at Indiana University in Bloomington, Indiana in the early-to-mid 1980s. I happened to drop in on a dormitory floor party, and I noticed that a female friend of mine was sloppy drunk, and these two male students were just totally manhandling her and on the verge of taking her somewhere to gang-rape her.

I intervened, which almost led to a fight between one of the two males and myself, but I ultimately led my friend out of harm's way and into her dormitory room.

The second instance involved a male friend of mine while we were leaving a nightclub late one Saturday night in Los Angeles in the late 1990s. There were two attractive women walking ahead of us, and one of the two women was sloppy drunk (she could barely stand up while she was walking). A few minutes later, my friend and I were in the parking garage, and the woman who was drunk began flirting with my friend. Next thing I knew, my friend began kissing her, and then my friend was on the verge of proceeding to intercourse with her right then and there in the parking garage until I intervened and stopped him. He and I exchanged some harsh words that night, but a few weeks later, he actually thanked me for preventing him from doing something that he knew would later regret.

I have never had sex with a woman for the very first time while she was fully inebriated or sloppy drunk, or when I knew ahead of time that a woman had heavy-duty (illegal) drugs in her system, such as cocaine or heroin. Never, ever. Even before the concept of 'date-rape' was a subject of mainstream news, I always avoided those situations.

There was at least one other time when I engaged in a heated argument with a former roommate of mine in Los Angeles because he let me know that he had purchased some *Rohypnol pills* (otherwise known as "Roofies" or "Date-Rape drugs"), and planned on using them with some women he had recently met. After our contentious conversation, I must have gotten through to him because he eventually decided to flush the pills down the toilet.

I have known some men who attempted to try to justify their use of drugs and/or alcoholic beverages with women by saying, *"It's not like I held a gun to the woman's head and forced her to drink liquor or forced her to smoke marijuana ... so how am I guilty of anything wrong?"*

I don't care if a woman enthusiastically VOLUNTEERS to drink multiple shots of Tequila or Vodka in your presence, or VOLUNTEERS to snort multiple lines of cocaine with you. **If a woman is not in the correct (sober) mental state to provide you with proper verbal (sexual) consent, then you need to avoid having sex with her. Especially if it is your very first time being with her in a physically intimate manner**.

Are there women who have falsely and invalidly accused men of date-raping them? Sure. It happened to the former high school football star **Brian Banks** (Google his story).

There is no such thing as a 100% guaranteed method of preventing false date-rape charges from a woman, but you should always make every effort to receive **verbal** (sexual) **consent** from a woman **while she is in a totally sober state of mind** before proceeding toward intercourse and/or oral sex or anal sex.

I know of at least two professional dating coaches who have been accused of exhibiting behavior that *bordered on* being categorized as date-rape.

You do not want to gain a reputation for being overly aggressive with women physically or gain a reputation for getting women drunk or high before you engage in sexual relations with him. This could very well result in you facing some legal consequences and repercussions in the long run.

## MEN WHO KIDNAP and TORTURE, RAPE, or MURDER NEW FEMALE ACQUAINTANCES

Date-Rape (also known as a "Acquaintance Rape") is when an act of sexual assault takes place between a man and a woman who are generally familiar with each other socially and have usually engaged in at least one or two conversations with each other before the act of sexual assault took place.

Even before the concept of date-rape came to the forefront of society in the early 1990s, a number of men for centuries had been charged with groping and/or sexually assaulting women who they had never talked to before or shared the woman's company in a social setting before.

Anytime you blend one part **misogyny** with two parts **sexual frustration**, dangerous behavior exhibited by men (sometimes referred to as "toxic masculinity") is likely to happen. This 'dangerous' behavior could include rape, assault and battery, kidnapping and torture, or even murder.

One group of men in *The Manosphere* who generally fall into the category of 'toxic masculinity' are those men known as "**homicidal & suicidal incels**." An *incel* is a man who is "involuntarily celibate" *(as opposed to a **monk**, who chooses to remain celibate indefinitely)* and has maintained a state of romantic and sexual frustration for a minimum of one year, and in some cases, five years or longer.

There are generally three types of *incels*. The first is the group I mentioned in the paragraph above (homicidal & suicidal incels). This group of sexually frustrated men reach a point where they feel so hopeless and so angry and bitter toward women, and particularly very beautiful and sexy women (who they often refer to as "Stacy" types), and the handsome, charming womanizer types that they feel these women gravitate toward (they often refer to these men as "Chad" types), that they are willing to commit murder, suicide, or a blend of both. One name of a man in this category would be **Elliot Rodger**.

The second group of incels just consistently dwell in a world of self-pity, defeatism, and pessimism. All they do is whine and complain about how disappointing and unsatisfying their love life, sex life, and social life is, and how the world is just totally messed up and favors only the handsome, charming, smooth and seductive 'Chad' type men.

The third and final group of incels are those who generally will seek out self-help advice from dating coaches, PUAs, and other assorted dating & relationship advice gurus, and they genuinely want to fully immerse themselves in activities that center on personal development and self-improvement.

Given that I have been working as a professional dating coach for approximately two decades, I have coached and consulted with a high number of men who fall into the latter of the three groups of *incel* types. These men are not necessarily angry or bitter toward women, nor do they possess any sort of homicidal and/or suicidal tendencies.

As far as the first two groups of incels, I have sometimes viewed blogs and discussion forums in *The Manosphere* where at least a small percentage of men from the first two groups of incels will express comments along the lines of, *"I feel as though women deserve to be groped and manhandled. Some might call that rape, but I don't. No man should ever be prevented from having sex for an indefinite number of years and have to resort to nothing more than constant masturbation!"*

The men who posted these comments were **totally serious** (i.e., no lighthearted emojis or smiley faces or "LOL" accompanied the comments).

Some men truly believe that they are more or less **entitled** to women's sexual companionship. These men literally believe that women were put on Planet Earth to please and satisfy the sexual needs and urges of horny heterosexual men like themselves, and that no man should feel obligated to ever seek out a woman's verbal (sexual) consent.

The reality is, **no man is entitled to share the company of a woman** in a physically intimate and sexual manner, and similarly, no woman is entitled to share the company of any particular man in a physically intimate and sexual manner.

Additionally, no woman owes a man her non-sexual attention and companionship, and **no man owes a woman his non-sexual time, attention, and companionship or access to his financial resources and materialistic possessions**.

Once again, I divide all methods of getting a woman to agree to have sex with a man into five general categories:

- **ATTRACTION**
- **(VERBAL) SEDUCTION**
- **DISHONESTY & MANIPULATION**
- **FINANCIAL NEGOTIATION**
- **COERCION & SEXUAL ASSAULT**

I fully endorse and recommend any method of **attraction** and/or **persuasion and verbal seduction**. I totally frown on any method of getting women in bed that involves blatantly dishonest behavior, disingenuous and misleading & manipulative behavior, and/or physically forceful or coercive behavior *(that could or could not include the use of drugs and/or alcoholic beverages)*.

Again, if your desire and aspiration is to become some sort of womanizing 'player,' then I only endorse and condone ethical womanizing that includes being upfront, specific, and straightforwardly honest with women about the fact that all you are really interested in is a few episodes of short-term and/or non-monogamous no-emotions-involved sex. This type of behavior falls within the parameters of my ***Mode One Approach*** philosophy.

Beginning with no later than the age of 22 up until now, I have never lied to a woman or resorted to manipulating a woman psychologically or emotionally to get her to agree to engage in sexual relations with me. Over the last 35 or 36 years, my primary pattern of behavior involves verbally communicating my sexual desires, interests, and intentions to women in an extremely confident, highly self-assured, upfront, specific, and unapologetic and straightforwardly honest manner.

***Mode One Baby. Make it happen.***

In Part Two of this book, I am going to spend the next five chapters discussing five specific types of women that I would recommend that you go out of your way to avoid entering into any sort of long-term, emotionally profound, strictly monogamous relationship with that has a high potential to eventually lead to marriage and children.

Continue reading my friend.

# PART TWO

## Women to Avoid as Long-Term Romantic Companions #1: Covert Gold Diggers

If you refer back to Chapter Three, there are some men I refer to as ***chumps***, ***simps***, and ***Mode Three Targets***. These are men who – for better or for worse – tend to attract attention from women who are shallow, superficial, and incredibly manipulative and highly materialistic due to the fact that these men are always emphasizing things such as their income, their expensive material possessions, their financial investments, and their net worth (assuming they are wealthy or on the verge of being wealthy).

Believe it or not, there are some men who thoroughly enjoy being used by women for their financial and materialistic generosity. These men are commonly referred to as either ***Sugar Daddy*** types or ***Financial Sponsors***, ***Paypigs*** and/or ***Financially Generous Cuckolds*** (BDSM), or simply ***Beta Male Providers***. Another type of man who falls into this category would be one who is the regular, semi-regular, or occasional client of a *street prostitute*, professional *Call Girl* or an upscale *Erotic Escort*. This type of man is known simply as a ***Trick***.

These types of men are open to women exploiting them for their generosity regarding their financial resources and materialistic possessions as long as they are rewarded with the guaranteed opportunity to share the company of these young, beautiful, sexually appealing women in a physically intimate and sexual manner.

A man who is known as a *chump*, a *simp*, or a *Mode Three Target* is not really in that category. Men who are *chumps*, *simps*, and *Mode Three Targets* are men who regularly get taken advantage of by manipulative and highly materialistic women **without fully or consciously realizing it**.

In simple terms, if you end up in a long-term relationship and/or marriage with a woman who is known to be a very shallow, superficial, manipulative and highly materialistic gold digger type, and you know she is this type of woman at the beginning of the long-term relationship (LTR) or marriage, then if you get fully exploited in a manner that ultimately leaves you financially bankrupt, **that is totally on you**. No other man is going to express any sympathy or empathy toward you.

If you pay close attention to the title of this chapter, it says "**Covert** Gold Diggers." A woman who makes it known from the beginning to a man who is her long-term boyfriend, fiancé, or husband that she is extremely materialistic and very high maintenance is usually referred to as a ***Sugar Baby*** type, or in the BDSM lifestyle, a ***Financial Dominatrix*** *(or simply 'Financial Dom' for short).*

On the other hand, there are a high number of women who end up with a very financially and materialistically generous boyfriend, fiancé, or husband that keep their highly materialistic and financial favor-seeking tendencies "undercover" and camouflaged from the general public.

These women will make it seem as though they are in a LTR with a man or married to a man because they genuinely 'love' him for his looks, his intelligence and his sense of humor, his love for children and family, and his sense of moral character and personal integrity.

In real blunt terms, these women are essentially *professional actresses*, only you will never see them in any feature films or television programs. Their acting performances happen in **real life** ... similar to the acting skills of a professional *con artist* or *undercover police detective*.

Realistically, the vast majority of men in society will never have to worry about whining and complaining about women who took advantage of them financially and materialistically because most men do not earn enough money to even attract the attention and companionship of a true top tier *Covert Gold Digger* type.

You have to realize … there is a big difference between a woman who simply operates as a *Manipulative Timewaster* type and a woman who operates as a top-notch, full-fledged, top tier *Covert Gold Digger* type.

For example, if you earn less than approximately one million (U.S.) dollars per year, 99% chance, you will never cross paths with a true top tier *Covert Gold Digger* type. I would say at bare minimum, you would have to be earning no less than approximately $200,000 (USD) per year to even remotely attract the attention and companionship of a *Covert Gold Digger* type.

Women who operate as *Covert Gold Digger* types could care less about a free lunch or free dinner at a five-star restaurant downtown. These women could care less if you were to purchase $1,500 worth of clothes for them or buy them a $2,000 gold bracelet.

No. Women who operate as true top tier *Covert Gold Digger* types are the type of women who do not pay for any of their month-to-month living expenses, such as rent or mortgage payments, automobile finance loan payments, vacation travel expenses, or any other regular financial obligation that helps support their high quality of life.

These women sometimes have careers that were essentially handed to them on a silver platter where they have to perform little or almost no real work.

To that point, when I lived in Los Angeles, in addition to some of the full-time permanent work I was able to secure, I also did a lot of "temporary employment" assignments at many of the feature-film and television studios in the Entertainment Industry between 1995 and 2000.

During many of my long-term temporary employment assignments, I would many times work with women who were either top tier *Covert Gold Digger* themselves, or at minimum, they were close friends with women who were in that category.

Here would be my description of the five tiers of *Covert Gold Digger* types:

**Top Tier** (Covert) **Gold Digger** – The woman's boyfriend, fiancé, or husband has a net worth of at least one million dollars, and she does not pay for any of her own month-to-month living expenses nor does she pay for any of her own material possessions. Many women who are the wives of very wealthy professional athletes fall into this category.

**Second Tier** (Covert) **Gold Digger** – The woman's boyfriend, fiancé, or husband earns a yearly income of no less than $200,000 per year (with very little financial debt or credit card debt), and he pays for just about all of the woman's month-to-month living expenses, clothing, and other material possessions.

**Third Tier** (Covert) **Gold Digger** – The woman is a *serial monogamist*, who regularly connects with affluent men for short-term romantic relationships. Often times, she operates as a discreet and covert professional *Call Girl* or *Erotic Escort* (but she never officially markets herself to men as a professional sex worker). This woman will allow men to engage in short-term and/or non-monogamous sex with her, but the price for her sexual companionship will usually be in the range of $1,000 per day or $3,500 or more for Thursday-thru-Sunday type weekend companionship.

**Fourth Tier** (Covert) **Gold Digger** – This is the type of woman I refer to in my other books as an *Erotic Hypocrite*. When this woman feels like a man is a self-assured, seductive, highly masculine *Alpha male* type, she will allow him to engage in short-term and/or non-monogamous sex with her for **FREE**, but if she perceives a man as being more of a *Beta male* type, then that man will have to offer her a number of free meals, monetary favors, and expensive materialistic gifts in order to engage in any variation of short-term and/or non-monogamous sexual relations with her.

**Bottom Tier** (Covert) **Gold Digger** – This is a woman who is simply your basic *Manipulative Timewaster* and *Financial Favor Seeker*. This woman will offer men ***The Possibility of Sex*** in exchange for free meals, free movie tickets, free concert tickets, free clothing items, and other assorted moderately expensive materialistic gifts. This type of woman will never, ever end up actually engaging in sexual relations with the men who are spending money on her though.

All of these types of women make sure that they take great care of their feminine figure, their health and fitness, their personal hygiene and grooming, and they generally try to always appear immaculate and eye-catching with their physical appearance.

They will invest time and effort socializing with affluent men just long enough to **size them up** and they will ultimately determine if one or more of these men are **a)** financially and materialistically generous with women, and **b)** a bit naïve and romantically and sexually frustrated, and desperate for the companionship of a woman who is young, very beautiful, and very sexually appealing.

Let's be real. If you are a man who is always bragging about the fact that you own a house on the beach, or the fact that you own both a *Jaguar F-Type Coupe* and a brand new *Range Rover*, then of course you are going to attract the attention of women who operate as *Covert Gold Digger* types.

If there is at least one benefit to being a man without means, it is that you never have to worry about attracting the attention of women who operate as *Covert Gold Digger* types.

Take me for example. From the time I was roughly 23 years of age, all the way up until I was about 41 or 42, I was always struggling financially. Many times during that period, I was either flat broke and/or unemployed for months.

At the risk of doing a bit of bragging though, I still was able to attract and seduce women who were anywhere from slightly above-average *(a "6" or "7" on most men's "1" to "10" scale of beauty and sex appeal)* to exceptionally beautiful *(an "8" or above on most men's "1" to "10" scale)*.

When I was in my twenties and thirties, I relied on a combination of my looks, my supreme level of confidence and heterosexual masculinity, and probably most importantly, my smooth, persuasively charming and ultra-seductive *mouthpiece*. I never, ever relied on offering women money, financial favors, or materialistic gifts because in very blunt terms, I did not have any of those things in my possession TO offer women.

I was able to engage in short-term and/or non-monogamous sex with many women without having to spend money on them or 'Wine & Dine' them, whereas a number of other men had to do just that as a prerequisite to engaging in sexual relations with these women.

If you meet a woman that you view as potential long-term girlfriend material or future wife material, never begin your social interactions with a woman offering to spend a lot of money on her or offering her expensive materialistic gifts *(many men in The Manosphere refer to that as "leading with your wallet")*. In the long-run, you would be setting yourself up to be played by a *Covert Gold Digger* type (refer back to Chapter Three if necessary).

When you are too quick to offer to spend money on women or too quick to offer women expensive materialistic gifts, it makes you look romantically and sexually **desperate**. Women are most turned on by men who they feel have **multiple options for female sexual companionship** (which is why many women are drawn to womanizing *player* types).

If you do happen to be a man with means *(i.e., you are earning a yearly salary of approximately $200,000 per year or higher and have a low degree of financial debt)*, take a few weeks or a few months to carefully 'vet' a woman to make sure she is not a highly materialistic, high maintenance *Covert Gold Digger* type looking to simply use you to subsidize her high quality lifestyle and expensive tastes.

Arguably the greatest detriment to entering into a LTR or marriage with a *Covert Gold Digger* type is that she is either **a)** going to cheat on you behind your back with men who are more physically attractive than you, more sexually appealing than you and possess better bedroom skills than you, and are generally more verbally smooth, persuasive, and seductive than you *(I will cover this in more detail in* ***Chapter Ten****)*, and/or **b)** will find another *chump*, *simp*, or ***Mode Three Target*** who is wealthier than you, easier to get along with than you, more flattering, entertaining, and emotionally empathetic than you, and more naïve and easier to manipulate than you, so consequently, she is going to **dump you** and enter into a LTR or marriage with that other *Mode Three Target*.

Some men in *The Manosphere* refer to situation "b" as *monkey branching*, which is a form of *female* ***hypergamy***.

Always, always, always remember and refer back to those three types of sexual interest I discussed in Chapter Three (between pages 51 and 59). *Covert Gold Digger* types can only offer you **Manipulative & Opportunistic sexual interest**. They will never, ever offer you *genuine sexual interest* (i.e., lust).

If you are a man who is totally fine with exchanging money, financial favors, employment offers and job promotions, and expensive materialistic gifts in exchange for the sexual (and non-sexual) companionship of a young, very beautiful, and very sexually appealing woman, be my guest. All I ask is that you do not later post comments on internet blog sites and discussion forums whining and complaining about how some gold digger took advantage of you and cleaned out your bank accounts leaving you financially bankrupt.

The primary man I am offering advice to in this particular chapter are those men who are searching for a woman who truly loves them for who they are as a person rather than finding a woman who simply wants to exploit them for what they have to offer financially and materialistically.

I know many men who are part of *The Manosphere* who believe non-materialistic women do not even exist. I vehemently disagree. I can give two examples from my own immediate family.

Number one, my late mother. My father was once unemployed for almost **two years**, but yet my mother did not leave him and divorce him. Instead, she temporarily became the 'bread winner' of the family for a period of 18-23 months. If my mother had been a *Covert Gold Digger* type, she would have dumped my father in that situation.

Another woman would be my sister-in-law, who is my older brother's wife. For the first few years of their relationship, my sister-in-law was earning *almost twice as much* in yearly income as my brother was. I know some women that would not even dare think of maintaining a long-term relationship or marriage with a man who earns significantly less than them.

Some men in *The Manosphere* believe that if you believe in the concept of "true love," this means that you possess a "Blue Pill" mentality and mindset. I disagree with these men who happen to maintain this very invalid belief.

I consider myself very much in possession of a "Red Pill" mentality and mindset, yet I still believe in the concept of 'true love' (the more real-life version of it, not the overly exaggerated version of it that is often portrayed in many Hollywood movies).

For those ignorant of these terms influenced by the 1999 action-thriller, *The Matrix*, to be **'Blue Pill'** means that you are a man who is generally ignorant and naïve to both the sexually duplicitous and adulterous ways of women as well as ignorant and naïve to the manipulative and materialistic tendencies of the average woman.

To be **'Red Pill'** means that you are fully aware of the fact that a high percentage of women have a tendency to be sexually duplicitous and romantically unfaithful, and you are fully aware that a high percentage of women are spoiled and demanding, and manipulative and materialistic.

Two additional "pills" that are discussed quite often among men who are part of *The Manosphere* would be men who are **'Purple Pill'** (i.e., you maintain a lot of Red Pill truths privately, but you publicly espouse a lot of Blue Pill oriented attitudes and advice) and men who are **'Black Pill'** (i.e., you maintain a very extreme variation of being *Red Pill*, and you essentially believe that all women are highly promiscuous and romantically unfaithful, all women are incorrigibly manipulative and materialistic, and no commitment to self-improvement or personal development activities *(such as losing weight or developing better social skills)* will help a man that women view as unattractive and sexually unappealing experience any higher degree of success with women.

I simply define 'true love' as a blend of **a)** an indefinite sense of **genuine sexual interest** *(i.e., lust)* combined with **b)** a genuine sense of **loyal, honest, trustworthy friendship** between a man and woman in a LTR or marriage. That's my formula.

**LUST + LOYAL FRIENDSHIP = TRUE LOVE**.

If there is too much lust in your LTR or marriage, but not enough friendship, 99% chance, that LTR or marriage is not going to last for too long. Similarly, if you have a great friendship with your girlfriend, fiancée, or wife, but there is not enough genuine sexual lust between you two, that LTR or marriage is going to result in a high degree of infidelity.

Bottom line? A man cannot **purchase** *true love* from a woman. Keep that in mind. Plain and simple, never allow a woman to '**sell**' you her long-term romantic companionship.

In the very next chapter, I will be discussing and describing women who love to 'steal' other women's boyfriends, fiancés, and husbands. I refer to these women as "**Man Thieves**."

Continue reading my friend.

## Women to Avoid as Long-Term Romantic Companions #2: Ambitious Side Chicks

Sometimes, I wish I had just one dollar for each time a woman has asked me, *"Alan, why do men cheat?"* One simple response I have offered to these women who have asked me that question is that women make it so damn easy for men to cheat on their wives, fiancées, and long-term romantic companions.

Fact: over the course of my adult life I have had more women aggressively offer me the opportunity to have sex with them during a period of time when I was romantically involved with a woman than I have during a period of time when I was single and free to date multiple women.

When you really think about it, that is a damn shame. Many of my male friends have told me that they have experienced the exact same thing with many women who they are acquainted with.

I know some men who have told me that once women found out that they were married, engaged to be married, or otherwise romantically involved with a woman, these scandalous women began making very aggressive sexual advances toward them.

Women are much different than men in a number of ways (but also similar to men in a number of ways). Generally speaking, the vast majority of men much prefer to engage in sexual relations with women who are single and unattached. Most men are far more likely to pursue a woman who is single and unattached than a woman who is married, engaged to be married, or otherwise romantically involved.

Many women, on the other hand, find men who are married, engaged to be married, or otherwise romantically involved to be much more appealing to them than a man who is single and unattached.

Even many of my closest female friends and female acquaintances have acknowledged this fact to me many times over the last 35 years. Many women's underlying attitude is this: if this man is capable of **pleasing and satisfying a woman in bed** multiple times consistently, then why hasn't any woman snatched him up yet and claimed him as her own?

Similarly, many women feel that if a man's **non-sexual** companionship is pleasant and entertaining, easy to get along with, and highly appealing to multiple women, then why hasn't any woman snatched him up yet and claimed him as her own?

In other words, many women feel that if both a man's *sexual* attention and companionship and his *non-sexual* attention and companionship is highly appealing, then there is no way that this man should be able to remain single and unattached indefinitely.

Many women feel that if a man remains single and unattached for too many months and/or too many years, that this generally means that something must be 'wrong' with him.

Here are a few of the assumptions that women maintain about a man if that man has remained single and unattached for too many months and/or too many years consecutively:

- He has less-than-average and less-than-satisfying bedroom skills
- If he is good in bed, he is totally untrustworthy and incorrigibly promiscuous and unfaithful
- He exhibits behavior that makes it hard to get along with him *(e.g., too dominant, too uncompromising, too argumentative, etc.)*
- He has a very boring personality and/or a very unappealing sense of humor
- He is secretly gay or bisexual
- He is lazy, unambitious, financially irresponsible, erratically employed, and/or broke and full of financial debt

At minimum, women expect men who are single and unattached to have a regular stable of dependable, available casual sex lovers. If a man is single for too long AND he is not some sort of womanizing player type, then women definitely feel as though something is 'wrong' with that man.

Famous comedian **Chris Rock** once had a funny comedy bit where he said, *"When men tell other men that they have a great woman in their life, their male friends and acquaintances will say, 'I want a woman* ***just like that****!' But when women tell other women that they have a great man in their life, that woman's female friends and acquaintances will say, 'I want* ***HIM****!'"*

Many women offer sex to men who are married, engaged to be married, or otherwise romantically involved with the hope of 'stealing away' that man from his current wife, fiancée, or long-term romantic companion. I refer to these women as ***Man Thieves*** *and/or* ***Ambitious Side Chicks***.

Some women are very competitive in this regard. Some women feel like, "Well, I am better looking than that man's wife ..." or "I bet I am more satisfying in bed than that man's fiancée ..."

There are a number of women who genuinely feel that men are very easy to influence and easy to manipulate with their beauty, their feminine sex appeal, and by offering men ***The Possibility of*** *(quick, easy, short-term, non-monogamous)* ***Sex***.

When a man who is married, engaged to be married, or otherwise romantically involved carries himself as if he is completely satisfied sexually by his wife, fiancée, or long-term romantic companion, a lot of women who are both *ambitious* and *competitive* will set their sights on that man, and they will not stop until they 'steal' that man away from his wife, fiancée, or long-term romantic companion.

If you own my book, ***Oooooh … Say it Again***, one of my most quoted comments in that book is "Pussy attracts More Pussy." It's just like money. There is a saying and belief that the more money you accumulate, the easier it will be to attract new opportunities to gain even more wealth.

Well, in my experience and observation, the same can be said for opportunities to engage in sexual relations with women. The more women believe that you are already capable of pleasing and satisfying one or more women in bed, the more likely they are to offer you the opportunity to exchange orgasms with them.

Have you ever engaged in sexual relations with a woman, and days later or weeks later, that woman's friend, roommate, co-worker, or even mother, daughter, sister or cousin began flirting with you in a subtle or even an overt manner? I refer to this as ***referral pussy***.

You pleased and satisfied Woman #1 in bed, and she decided to 'kiss & tell' with one or more women who are close to her, and she sang the praises of your satisfying bedroom skills. Now, these other women are curious and intrigued about you, and they want you to please and satisfy THEM.

On the flip side, if you engage in sexual relations with a woman, and you leave that woman feeling disappointed, unsatisfied, and sexually frustrated … you're in trouble. Nine times out of ten, that woman is going to tell all of her girlfriends and close female acquaintances that you suck in bed. Consequently, once that happens, the best you can hope for is a purely platonic friendship with those women who know about your less-than-desirable bedroom skills.

This brings me back to the appeal of men who have a wife, a fiancée, or a long term romantic companion. When women assume that you have at least one woman in your life that you are satisfied with sexually, and that is satisfied with you sexually, then women who are ambitious and competitive are going to make every effort to share your company socially as much as possible.

On top of that, if you are reasonably handsome, financially self-sufficient, fairly charismatic and personable, and the women you come in contact with generally consider you a man who is very easy to get along with, then women who are ambitious and competitive are going to make every effort to share your company in an attempt to 'steal' you away from your wife, fiancée, or long-term romantic companion.

Make no mistake: some men who are married, engaged to be married, or otherwise romantically involved actually welcome this type of flattering and flirtatious attention from other women.

If you are a long-time follower and supporter of mine, then you already know how I feel about cheating and adultery. I despise men and women who cheat on their spouses and other long-term romantic companions. I believe cheating and adultery is an act of cowardice, and even more so, I believe it is simply **unethical** and **just plain wrong**.

More often than not, one or more episodes of adultery and infidelity will open the door for 'unnecessary drama' to seep into your marriage or long-term relationship. On the positive end, beginning with the age of 22, I have never been a man who has a history of cheating on women, but on the down side, I have been guilty of engaging in sexual relations with women who were at the time married, engaged to be married, or otherwise romantically involved with another man. I will go into more detail about this in **Chapter Ten**.

A good number of men typically are naïve about the ambition and competitiveness of their favorite mistress (if married) or 'side piece' (if unmarried). Many men believe that these side chicks will be indefinitely content with remaining a man's mistress or side piece. In most cases, this is not true.

Realistically, at least half of the women who initially offer themselves to a man as a potential long-term mistress or 'side piece' ultimately aspire to **replace** that man's wife, fiancée, or long-term romantic companion. Again, this is why I refer to these types of women as ***Man Thieves*** *and* ***Ambitious Side Chicks***.

Ambitious and competitive side chicks who operate as *Man Thieves* will initially give naïve and unsuspecting men the misleading impression that they do not mind sharing that man with his wife, fiancée, or long-term romantic companion. In reality though, these women are devising a plan to ruin that man's marriage, engagement, or LTR.

Did any of you reading this book ever watch the 1987 suspense thriller titled ***Fatal Attraction***? In this film, Actress Glenn Close plays the character of *Alex Forrest*, who is a single woman who suffers from what is known as **Borderline Personality Disorder** (BPD).

Alex makes herself available for adulterous sex with a married lawyer named *Dan Gallagher* (played by Actor Michael Douglas). Dan seems to be under the misguided impression that he and Alex are just going to engage in a one-time sexual weekend fling.

Initially, Dan does not fully realize that Alex is mentally and emotionally compromised (read: crazy as hell; psychotic) and he does not realize that Alex is essentially a *Man Thief*.

I do not want to give away too many movie 'spoilers' for those who have yet to watch the film, but as the story of the film unfolds, you are able to see that Alex ultimately wants to eliminate Dan's wife, *Beth Gallagher* (Actress Anne Archer), and replace her in Dan's life.

Many times, when you engage in just a handful of erotic trysts with a mistress or 'side piece,' it may (initially) seem innocent and non-threatening to your marriage, engagement, or LTR.

Now, if you are in a situation where you are genuinely unsatisfied with the sexual and/or non-sexual component of your marriage, engagement, or long-term romantic relationship, then you need to sit down with your wife, fiancée, or long-term romantic companion and engage in a very candid, frank, unapologetically honest conversation about the problems you have identified with your spouse or romantic companion.

After that conversation happens, if you and your spouse or romantic companion cannot seem to arrive at a mutually agreed upon solution to the problems that plague your marriage or LTR, then unfortunately, it might be time to call it quits.

Then, once you are single and unattached again, you will be free to start dating and engaging in sexual relations with any woman who you choose to.

On the other hand, if you have a really great woman in your life as a wife, fiancée, or long-term romantic companion, then you need to really guard yourself against the temptation of quick, easy sex from other ambitious, competitive, and flirtatious women who want to 'steal' you away from your significant other.

First piece of advice: you should never talk about the problems you may be experiencing with your wife, fiancée, or long-term romantic companion with other people, and particularly, a man who might be sexually attracted to your female companion, or a woman that may be heavily attracted to you. Choosing to do either would be a **huge mistake** in the long-run.

You should never, ever give any other woman the impression that your wife, fiancée, or girlfriend is not satisfying all of your sexual desires, needs and fantasies. Once you do that, you will give a woman all of the motivation she needs to develop a strategy to attempt to lure you away from your spouse or romantic companion.

If you do indeed become guilty of this poor decision, then right there, you have potentially opened the door for a woman who is operating as a *Man Thief* to begin executing her plan to win you over, and attempt to 'steal' you away from your wife, fiancée, or long-term romantic companion. You would be playing right into her hands.

As a man, you have to ask yourself, would you want your wife or girlfriend telling a male friend or male acquaintance of hers that you leave her feeling sexually frustrated and unsatisfied, or that you leave her feeling bored or taken for granted and underappreciated? Of course not.

Once your wife, fiancée, or long-term romantic companion shares that type of information with another (heterosexual) man, more-than-likely he is either going to begin making plans to 'steal' her away from you, or at minimum, he will begin engaging in sexual relations with her behind your back.

I cannot speak for other men, but if a woman offers me sex while I am married, engaged to be married, or otherwise romantically involved, I will never, ever again view that woman as potential long-term girlfriend material or future fiancée and wife material.

What is very interesting and ironic to me is that it seems as though the more a man presents himself to a woman as a good, monogamous and romantically faithful husband, fiancé, or boyfriend, the more it seems many women want to tempt and persuade that man to cheat on his wife, fiancée, or long-term romantic companion. It is as if many women say to themselves, "If he has remained loyal to HER … he will surely remain loyal to ME if I am able persuade him to leave her for me."

Over the years, I have had a number of women openly confess to me that at least once or twice in their life, they pursued a man who was happily married, engaged to be married, or completely satisfied with his long-term romantic companion simply because they viewed it as some sort of 'competitive challenge.'

In other words, they wanted to see if they had the beauty, the sex appeal, and persuasive and seductive charm to 'steal' a man away from his loving wife, his loving fiancée, or his loving long-term girlfriend.

Once a man gives a woman even a mild impression that he is open to cheating on his wife, fiancée, or long-term romantic companion, women who are ambitious and competitive side chicks who operate as *Man Thieves* are going to begin pursuing them **relentlessly**.

Referencing the movie *Fatal Attraction* once again, if the potential mistress or side piece who begins pursuing you happens to be mentally and emotionally unstable, then this woman might be capable of doing **anything** to 'steal' you away from your wife, fiancée, or long-term romantic companion.

For example, this *Man Thief* might go as far as to develop a friendship with your wife, fiancée, or long-term girlfriend. Even more so, she might begin confessing to your significant other that you have been sexually intimate with her in a bold attempt to ruin your marriage, engagement or LTR.

Even worse, if she is truly crazy, she might threaten your wife, fiancée, or long-term girlfriend with physical harm (or even murder). You just never know.

I strongly believe that the media needs to be more harshly critical of women who choose to engage in sexual relations with men who are married, engaged to be married, or otherwise romantically involved.

The vast majority of the time, it seems as though many factions of the mainstream media only harshly criticize adulterous and unfaithful men rather than the women who openly pursue them and make themselves sexually available to these men. In my opinion, that is sexist and one-sided.

Think about it. If each and every woman in society were to choose to only engage in sexual relations with a man who was her husband, fiancé, or long-term boyfriend … or choose to only engage in sexual relations with a man who was single and unattached … then adultery and infidelity would come to an end virtually overnight.

In fairness to women though, many women could argue the exact same thing in reverse. If each and every heterosexual man in society were to choose to only engage in sexual relations with a woman who was his wife, fiancée, or long-term girlfriend … or at minimum, only choose to engage in sexual relations with women who were single and unattached … then women would argue that adultery and infidelity could come to an end virtually overnight.

Believe it or not, I truly believe – hypothetically – that if all heterosexual men in the world were to only limit themselves to engaging in sexual relations with their wife, fiancée, or long-term girlfriend only, many women would go nuts.

If you recall in my 2012 eBook version of ***The Possibility of Sex***, I briefly discussed when I was a part of this cult-like church between July 1994 and December 1996 when I resided in Los Angeles. The way the church was structured, any form of premarital sex or sex outside the context of marriage in general was strictly prohibited among the members of the church.

If a man who was a member of this church got caught engaging in sexual relations with a woman that wasn't his wife, he could be potentially dismissed from the church's membership and be shamed by the entire congregation of the church.

Because just about all the men in the church never pursued any of the women in the church for premarital sex or any form of short-term and/or non-monogamous 'casual' sex, guess what? Many of the women in the church became incredibly irritated, frustrated, and **sexually aggressive**!

One time, all of the unmarried men who were members of the church got called to attend an "Emergency Meeting of The Male Singles." My roommates and I just knew that this meeting would result in many of the men being admonished for making the mistake of being too sexually flirtatious with some of the female members of the church.

Wrong! The leaders of the meeting ended up discussing just the opposite situation. They basically warned us that a lot of the women in the church were guilty of exhibiting behavior that was very **sexually aggressive** toward the men while other women were literally *begging men to propose marriage to them* so that they could engage in sexual relations as soon as possible. This literally **blew my mind** at the time.

Also, in the 2012 eBook version of ***The Possibility of Sex***, I discussed an interaction I had with a very beautiful and very sexually appealing Latin woman who left this very same church. A few weeks after she abruptly ended her membership with the church, I happened to run into her while out running errands. She and I engaged in a brief conversation regarding her decision to leave the church.

When I asked her reasons for leaving the church, she replied, *"Alan, I am going to be blunt and honest. My ego couldn't handle not being pursued by men for (casual) sex. I had a few men that pursued me as a potential wife, but I did not have any men who pursued me for (casual) sex only."*

I said to this woman, "Well, we both know that premarital sex and casual sex was off limits in the church. Surely, you knew that. So why would you have expected any of the men to pursue you for short-term non-monogamous 'casual' sex?"

She replied, *"I am a woman. You are a man. You will never understand. I am a woman with a very healthy ego, and at the risk of coming across as very conceited and full of myself, before I joined the church, I had dozens of men pursuing me for (casual) sex on a weekly basis. On a weekly basis! And* ***I had my way with these men!*** *Alan, the thing about us women is, even if we are totally not interested in having sex with a particular man,* ***we still want that man to pursue us for (casual) sex****. Any woman who says otherwise is a blatant liar."*

In other words, this Latin woman was basically offering the basis for why many women are *Manipulative Timewasters*.

You see, if all men in society were to suddenly stop pursuing women for short-term and/or non-monogamous 'casual' sex, then women who operate as *Manipulative Timewasters* would become **incredibly frustrated**. Why? Because they would no longer be able to 'run game' on naïve and horny men and exploit those men for their **financial and materialistic generosity** nor would they be able to exploit men for indefinite access to their **non-sexual** time, attention, and companionship.

Most women love to have their way with (heterosexual) men, and even more so, many women **expect to** have their way with the vast majority of men that they come in contact with *(especially if these women are young, very beautiful, and extremely sexually appealing)*.

In my very next chapter, I am going to discuss and describe women who are, at minimum, a combination of spoiled and argumentative, and at maximum, are mentally and emotionally unstable.

Most men refer to these types of women as "**Drama Queens**" (other nicknames are "**Spoiled Diva**" types and "**Psycho Bitches**"). You never want a woman like this to become your wife, fiancée, or long-term romantic companion. Trust me on this.

Continue reading my friend.

## Women to Avoid as Long-Term Romantic Companions #3: Spoiled Drama Queens

If you were to identify all the personality characteristics of the women who I described in Chapter One, Chapter Two, Chapter Three, Chapter Six, and Chapter Seven … and blend all of those characteristics together and incorporate them into the mind and body of one woman, that one woman could be categorized as a ***Drama Queen*** or a ***Spoiled Diva***. If the woman also happens to be very *mentally and emotionally unstable* and *physically violent*, then some men would probably refer to her more so as a ***Psycho Bitch***.

The women who I am going to be discussing and describing in this chapter tend to exhibit behavior that goes a bit beyond just being a seasoned and savvy *Manipulative Timewaster* type and/or a *Covert Gold Digger* and potential *Man Thief* type.

At minimum, the women who I will be discussing and describing in this chapter are women who regularly exhibit behavior that is extremely **spoiled,** and they have a very bad habit of **nagging men** and **provoking verbal fights and unnecessary arguments with men**.

At maximum, the women who I will be discussing and describing in this chapter are women who are very mentally and emotionally unstable, which could lead to them **stalking men**, **vandalizing men's material possessions**, **threatening men with physical harm**, **physically assaulting men**, or in some very extreme cases, even **murdering men**.

In the same way you have a number of men who have been accused of being guilty of exhibiting behavior that could validly be described as "toxic masculinity" (reference Chapter Five), the women who I will be discussing and describing in this chapter *(as well as Chapter **Nine** and Chapter **Ten**)* have been accused of exhibiting behavior that could validly be described by men as ***toxic femininity***.

The reality: most men who work hard at their jobs and manage their finances in a responsible manner simply want to come home from work, eat dinner, drink a beer or other beverage, watch television and enjoy some peace of mind.

The vast majority of men do not wish to be nagged and they do not wish to engage in unnecessary arguments with their wife, fiancée, or long-term romantic companion if they can help it.

Anytime you as a man happen to be in a relationship with a woman who is always nagging you and/or she consistently attempts to bait you into engaging in a high number of unnecessary and highly contentious arguments with her, this means you are involved in a marriage or LTR with a woman who is a *Drama Queen* or *Spoiled Diva*.

Personally, I have experienced at least two former girlfriends who were legitimate *Drama Queen* and *Spoiled Diva* types. What was interesting was that at least one of those two ex-girlfriends of mine once openly admitted and acknowledged to me that she was a *Drama Queen*.

Her exact words to me were, *"I get bored with men **if there is no drama** in my romantic relationships."*

No joke. My ex-girlfriend actually said that to me. At least I give her points for blunt honesty. To this day, I cannot think of any other former girlfriend of mine who I engaged in as many unnecessary arguments with than this particular ex-girlfriend of mine. We argued over some of the most trivial and silliest of things. The sex was pretty good though.

What is usually the starting point for a woman who exhibits the behavior of a *Drama Queen* or *Spoiled Diva*? In my opinion, there are at least five (5) major behavioral components that will ultimately lead women to exhibit the behavior of a *Drama Queen* or *Spoiled Diva*.

Some of the characteristics and traits of women who are *Drama Queens* and *Spoiled Divas* have already been covered in the previous chapters of this book. Here is my assessment of many of the Top 5 psychological and behavioral traits of women who tend to exhibit the behavior of a *Drama Queen* or *Spoiled Diva*:

1) These women love to be **flattered excessively** *(reference Chapter One)*. These women constantly love to have their sense of beauty and sex appeal validated by men on a weekly, daily, or even hourly basis;

2) These women are very '**thin-skinned**' *(i.e., emotionally sensitive to criticisms and insults)* who never like to be criticized by anyone, or have the flaws and weaknesses of their personality and overall behavior identified and exposed … particularly by a man who they are married to or in a LTR with. They want compliments … or nothing;

3) These women have a very low tolerance for boredom *(reference Chapter Two)*. I mean, these women literally hate being bored for more than 5 or 10 minutes at a time. **They want to be constantly entertained** *(these women consider contentious arguments with men as a form of 'entertainment')*;

4) Similar to Trait #1 and Trait #3, **these women cannot stand to be temporarily or indefinitely ignored** by either a man who they find physically attractive and sexually appealing, or by a man who they feel they can easily control, influence, and manipulate. These women need **constant attention**;

5) Beginning with their pre-teen years, **these women were not disciplined or punished enough for the defiant, disrespectful, inappropriate, and/or undesirable behavior that they exhibited toward others**. Their mother, step-mother, father, step-father, siblings and other relatives, close friends, and former sexual lovers and romantic companions gave their 'bad behavior' a very lenient "pass," so now they never expect to experience any major consequences or repercussions for their undesirable behavior toward others

Let us start with Trait #1. Again, for this trait, all you have to do is go back and reference **Chapter One** in this book. As mentioned already, many men are guilty of *fawning over women* when their number one objective is to prevent, avoid, delay, or 'soften the blow' of rejection.

If you are a man who falls into this category, you play right into the hands of a woman who is a *Drama Queen* or *Spoiled Diva* type.

Many women who are exceptionally beautiful and possess an exceptionally high degree of sex appeal have been socialized to believe that they can literally use their looks and sex appeal to have their way with any man they come in contact with.

These women have come to expect multiple men (particularly, accommodating and emotionally empathetic *Beta male* types) to be at their beck and call constantly, ready to flatter them on demand at their request.

I will momentarily skip over Trait #2 and go to Trait #3. In the same way Trait #1 relates to everything I discussed in Chapter One, Trait #3 relates to just about everything I discussed in Chapter Two and Chapter Four.

There are many women who will maintain a large roster of purely platonic male friends solely for the purpose of having someone to talk to them and entertain them when they are feeling bored and/or lonely. I've known many women like this in my life over the years.

One of the reasons why morning and afternoon *Soap Opera* dramas on television are so popular is because of women who hate to be bored. Generally speaking, women watch more television dramas than men do. Men are more prone to watch sports-related shows or news-related shows on television.

Trait #3 leads right into Trait #4. When a woman hates being bored, she automatically also hates being ignored by those who are capable of flattering her ego, those who are capable of making her smile, giggle, or outright laugh, and those who are capable of providing her with some very pleasurable and satisfying orgasms. Again, these women also hate being ignored by the men they love to argue with.

Trait #2 and Trait #5 go hand-in-hand with one another. The primary reason why women who are *Drama Queen* and *Spoiled Diva* types hate to be criticized or admonished is because from the time they were very young, they had very few people in their life actually take the time to seriously check them on their spoiled and disrespectful behavior.

This plays into the delineation between men who are the proverbial "nice guy" type and men who are the proverbial "bad boy" or "jerk" type.

One of the primary reasons why many women will allow a 'bad boy' or 'jerk' type to engage in short-term and/or non-monogamous sexual relations with them, but only relegate the 'nice guy' type to either long-term relationship sex or worse, platonic friendship only, is because women get turned on by men who have the balls and backbone to put them in their place when they exhibit defiant, disrespectful and undesirable behavior in general.

Women don't mind being put in their place by a man who they perceive to be a strong, confident, very masculine and dominant *Alpha male* type. Conversely though, women absolutely despise being criticized or admonished by a man who they perceive to be a more lenient, accommodating, flattering, entertaining, non-confrontational, and passive and emotionally empathetic *Beta male* type.

For women who are *Drama Queen* and *Spoiled Diva* types, they have had many men – and in particular, *Beta male* type men – who were enamored by their beauty and sex appeal allow them to get away with behaving a like a **spoiled brat** or a flat-out **bitch**.

There are a number of women who have never been scolded or admonished by a man in their entire adult life. I am talking **never, ever**.

Their father or step-father never put them in check. Their uncles or grandfathers never put them in check. Their brothers or male cousins never put them in check, and none of their ex-boyfriends or former husbands ever put them in check.

The end result is these lenient and passive men in this woman's life have unintentionally contributed to her growing up to become an ultra-spoiled, highly demanding, and very controlling **bitch**.

The tricky thing with these women, is that more often than not, if you are a *Beta male* type who they have targeted either for **a)** marriage, **b)** a long-term romantic relationship (LTR), or **c)** a long-lasting purely platonic friendship, these women will rarely if ever reveal the spoiled, demanding, and argumentative side of their personality in their early interactions with you. Nope.

Being the savvy manipulators that they are, initially, they will present themselves as the most sweet, pleasant, easy-to-get-along-with woman you could ever meet in your life.

Then once these women have ensnared you into their trap, they will perform a behavioral "**bait and switch**" maneuver on you.

Many times, women like this do not reveal their real side to you until **after** you have exchanged wedding vows with them, or at minimum, after you have already impregnated them.

Some athletes often have expressed that they hate losing, but I think losing in sports teaches grade school, middle school, high school, and college-aged men and women one very valuable life lesson, which is that **you are not always going to have everything go your way, sometimes your ego is going to be bruised, sometimes your feelings are going to be hurt, and you are not always going to achieve each and every goal and objective that you strongly desire to**.

If any woman grew up in an environment where everyone around her always allowed her to have her way and always allowed her to get away with 'bad' behavior, that woman is going to develop a very **spoiled** and extremely **narcissistic** mentality.

I have maintained the belief for years that a child who is constantly allowed to get away with extremely spoiled behavior will more-than-likely grow up to become an adult who will be unable to handle the challenges and unexpected episodes of adversity that the real world will present to him or her.

Then, these same types of men and women will develop the potential to transition into becoming **psychopaths** and/or **sociopaths** who wreak havoc on society. Poor parenting is one factor that opens the door for crazy people to do damage in the world.

Men and women who are extremely spoiled and narcissistic literally believe the world revolves around them. They believe all circumstances in their life's experiences should work out in their favor.

I remember when I interviewed this guest on my audio podcast program titled ***Upfront & Straightforward with Alan Roger Currie*** (which was on the BlogTalkRadio platform) by the name of Steve Penner.

At one point during the interview, Penner was discussing women who fall into the category of what he described as "Former Beauty Queen" types (former Talk Radio show Host Tom Leykis would refer to these same women as "Former Hotties").

Penner said that these types of women have the hardest time transitioning from their twenties and thirties into their forties, fifties, and sixties because as they get older, the amount of flattering attention and monetary favors that they are accustomed to receiving from men (and in particular, *Beta male* types) tends to diminish **significantly**.

Many of these women cannot handle that mentally and emotionally. These women have grown accustomed to men who have been willing to spoil them and acquiesce to their demands on a regular basis, and now, none of those men are around.

The root of many women's sense of confidence and self-esteem is how beautiful they feel they are, how sexually appealing their feel they are, and how much their looks and sex appeal motivates men to give them **FREE, INDEFINITE ACCESS** to both the men's **non-sexual** time, attention, and companionship as well as the men's **financial resources** and **material possessions**.

For the most part, heavy duty manipulation and gold digging is a young woman's game. Once a woman hits the age of forty and older, her ability to manipulate a high number of men with her looks and/or sex appeal begins to diminish with each year they grow older, and many women cannot handle this mentally and emotionally.

Even a young woman who is a spoiled, nagging, extremely antagonistic and argumentative, and attention hungry *Drama Queen* and *Spoiled Diva* is going to be a turn-off for the vast majority of men.

Multiply that effect times five or ten for women who are forty years of age and older. What man in his right mind wants to grow old with a woman who is a grouchy, grumpy, highly spoiled (older) **bitch**?

If I had to criticize members of my own gender, it would be that a lot of men have often told me, *"Well Alan, I don't like to scold or admonish a woman who I am in a relationship or marriage with. I would rather say nothing than to indulge in an unnecessary argument with her."* Yeah, right.

I am never going to knowingly contribute to a woman maintaining the attitude and behavior of a *Drama Queen* or *Spoiled Diva*. Never.

I prefer not to date women who make me feel like I have to walk on eggshells because they are so 'thin-skinned' and emotionally sensitive. Hell, I do not even like maintaining platonic friendships with other men who are very 'thin-skinned' and emotionally sensitive.

There are too many people in society that go to extremes not to be perceived as rude, impolite, crass, insulting, offensive and/or disagreeable by others. These men and women then slowly but surely transition from being considered "well-mannered and polite" into becoming **blatant liars** and **disingenuous and misleading manipulators**.

Finally, the main sub-category of *Drama Queens* and *Spoiled Divas* that as a man you need to be the most wary of and even afraid of are the women who are not only spoiled and argumentative, but they are **mentally and emotionally unstable** and **physically violent**. These are the women I refer to as ***Psycho Bitches***.

If you recall, in the very last chapter – Chapter Seven – I mentioned the 1987 film titled ***Fatal Attraction*** starring Actor Michael Douglas as the married Beta male *Dan Gallagher* and Actress Glenn Close as his obsessive stalker, *Alex Forrest*.

Alex Forrest was a prime example of a woman that was BOTH **a)** an *Ambitious Side Chick* a.k.a. *Man Thief* and **b)** a *Drama Queen* and *Psycho Bitch*.

Women in real life who exhibit behavior that is similar to the fictional character of Alex Forrest are just not normal, and more-than-likely, they are mentally and emotionally unstable. The fictional character of Alex Forrest suffered from what is known as ***Borderline Personality Disorder*** (BPD).

There are actually **ten** different personality disorders that most psychiatrists and psychologists diagnose and discuss regularly. The other nine are:

**Antisocial Personality Disorder**
**Avoidant Personality Disorder**
**Dependent Personality Disorder**
**Histrionic Personality Disorder**
**Narcissistic Personality Disorder**
**Obsessive-Compulsive Personality Disorder**
**Paranoid Personality Disorder**
**Schizoid Personality Disorder**
**Schizotypal Personality Disorder**

In my adult life, I have had social interactions with at least a half dozen women who suffered from one or more of those ten personality disorders, and in addition, I have interacted with a number of women who suffered from some variation of **manic depression** and/or **Bipolar disorder**.

Many men make the mistake of allowing themselves to become so enamored by a woman's beauty and sex appeal that they place very little emphasis on closely examining a woman's **non-physical attributes** and personality traits.

Some men are under the mistaken impression that only women who are physically unattractive and/or sexually unappealing are those who are prone to stalk men. Not true at all. I have had women in my life who ended up being obsessive stalker types that were very beautiful and extremely sexy.

If you are currently married, engaged to be married, or otherwise romantically involved with a woman, and you feel as though she may be displaying signs and symptoms of one or more of the ten personality disorders, do not hesitate to encourage your significant other to seek professional help.

Cohabiting with a woman who possesses one or more of the ten personality disorders (or manic depression and/or Bipolar disorder) would be a major challenge for any man in the long-run.

One lighthearted comment I have heard many men in *The Manosphere* express is, *"Women who are Psycho Bitches are typically the kinkiest and most passionate lovers in bed!!"* Why of course they are. Their behavior is primarily guided by their emotions. **Extreme emotions** to be more specific.

The flip side to them being extremely kinky and passionate in bed is that they are insanely **jealous**, **possessive**, and **controlling**. These types of women are likely to totally flip out on a man if that man begins to ignore them or begins to shower another woman with more flattering attention than them.

This is why I have such a strong disdain for trivial *small talk*, *chit chat*, and *fluff talk*. That type of inconsequential conversation does not allow you to provoke a woman's **real side** (and/or crazy side) to reveal itself. I only like to engage in conversations with women that have the potential to neutralize any and all of a woman's ***disingenuous façades***.

Here are the common characteristics and early detectable signs and symptoms of women who will eventually end up exhibiting the behavior of a *Drama Queen*, *Spoiled Diva*, and/or *Psycho Bitch*:

Number one, the woman has a hard time sharing your company and remaining silent for more than ten minutes. She always wants to talk and/or listen to you talk. Remember that woman I discussed in Chapter Two who I used to travel on the commuter train from Northwest Indiana to Chicago with? She had this characteristic. It literally drove her crazy if we went too long without talking to each other.

Number two, any time a woman gives off signs that she seems to be very egotistically insecure about her looks, her sex appeal, her age, and/or the overall appeal of her personality and romantic companionship, then nine times out of ten, this woman is or will soon transition into becoming a *Drama Queen* and/or a *Psycho Bitch*.

Number three, any time a woman gives off signs that she is very 'thin-skinned' and emotionally sensitive in response to receiving harsh criticisms and stern admonishments from you and others, then nine times out of ten you are dealing with a woman who is or will soon transition into becoming a *Drama Queen*, *Spoiled Diva*, and/or *Psycho Bitch*.

Number four, the woman very frequently talks to you in a very condescending manner, and generally treats you as if you are some sort of personal servant or subordinate employee of hers.

Finally, when you refuse to allow the woman to maintain a highly spoiled attitude and you refuse to allow her to dominate your behavior regularly and/or disrespect you consistently, the woman tends to **physically assault you** or at minimum, **she threatens to** physically assault you. LEAVE THIS BITCH. NOW. SERIOUSLY. This definitely means you are dealing with a woman who not only is a *Drama Queen* or *Spoiled Diva* type, but this woman is even more so a *Psycho Bitch* type.

Warning: When you threaten to divorce this type of woman, break up with this type of woman, or indefinitely ignore this type of woman, this woman might threaten to **a)** commit suicide and/or murder or **b)** vandalize some of your material possessions and seek some sort of 'vengeance' against you in some manner, such as revealing disparaging details about your personal life to the general public. Keep this in mind. These women are literally **dangerous**.

In my very next chapter, I am going to be discussing and describing yet another type of woman who is guilty of 'toxic femininity' in the very worst way. The women I am going to be discussing are ***Closet Misandrists***. These women have a passionate **hatred for men**, but they will never reveal that reality to you in your early interactions with them.

Continue reading my friend.

## .Women to Avoid as Long-Term Romantic Companions #4: Closet Misandrists

**Misogynist** and **Misandrist**.

If you are not already familiar with these two terms, I am going to make you familiar with them right now.

Many men would argue that the first of the two terms above is used too much and inappropriately, while the second of the two terms above is not used **nearly enough** by various factions of the mainstream media as well as by women themselves.

A *misogynist* is a man who maintains a passionate disdain for the entire female gender. In most cases, this type of man literally hates and despises any and all women.

If he is heterosexual, a *misogynist* might still engage in sexual relations with women from time to time (particularly, with *street prostitutes*, professional *Call Girls*, and upscale *Erotic Escorts*), but in general, he despises women and does not respect them as human beings.

A *misogynist* will usually make every effort to avoid socially interacting with women in any sort of non-physical, non-sexual, purely platonic manner

UNLESS they have a strong desire to harshly criticize a group of women, insult them, and generally antagonize them.

Most of the men who I have already discussed and described in **Chapter Five** would fall into the category of a *misogynist*.

The main problem with this term, is that many women and some factions of the mainstream media tend to "over-use" this term and/or use it in an invalid or inappropriate manner.

For example, just because a man expresses some degree of criticisms of various aspects of women's behavior does not automatically mean that he deserves the label of *misogynist*.

More specifically, just because a man occasionally refers to women who behave in a very disrespectful and/or physically violent manner toward him as "bitches" *(see Chapter Eight)* does not automatically qualify him to be categorized as a *misogynist*.

I could go on and on. Are you familiar with the name Ted Bundy? Bundy was one of this nation's most notorious serial killers of women. You see, Ted Bundy was a true *misogynist*. Same with the aforementioned Elliot Rodger.

Both Bundy and Rodger had so much bitterness and resentment toward women that they literally wanted to physically harm and murder women. This represents the most extreme form of **misogyny**.

One reason why the mainstream media does not focus on women who are *misandrists* as much as they do men who are *misogynists* is because men are more known for raping women, physically assaulting women, and murdering women much more than vice versa.

It is extremely rare for a woman who is a *misandrist* to become a serial killer of men in the same way Ted Bundy was a serial killer of women. Another reason is that many factions of Corporate America, and in particular, mainstream media and the Entertainment Industry, are dreadfully afraid of pissing off women. Women as a group spend more money on consumer items than men do as a group, and they also invest more time watching television and movies than men do as a group.

I have always told friends, acquaintances, and clients that there is a big difference between a *chauvinist*, a *sexist*, and a *misogynist*. A lot of women tend to lump all three of those categories of men together, and use each of those three terms interchangeably, which for a pedantic person like myself, is highly irritating and a huge mistake.

A **chauvinist** (which can be either a man or a woman) is a person who believes that members of each gender should always maintain certain "traditional roles" when it comes to marriage as well as when it comes to the professional workplace.

An example of a ***male*** *chauvinist* would be a man who believes that all men should always be the more dominant partner in a marriage or LTR, and that all women should always be the partner who regularly prepares meals and keeps the household clean and organized.

An example of a ***female*** *chauvinist* would be a woman who believes that women should never make the first move to invite a man to join them on a lunch date or dinner date, and she also firmly believes that men should always pay for her meal at the conclusion of a lunch date or dinner date.

A man can very well exhibit the behavior of a *chauvinist* without also exhibiting the behavior of a *misogynist*. Same with a woman. A woman can be a *chauvinist* without necessarily being a *misandrist*.

A **sexist** (which also can be either a man or a woman) is a person who exhibits behavior that is very prejudiced and discriminatory toward members of the opposite gender.

An example of a ***male** sexist* would be a man who only hires men to fulfill the most important and high-paying careers for the company he owns and manages, but he regularly relegates women to only being hired as administrative assistants, secretaries, and other low-paying auxiliary positions.

An example of a ***female** sexist* would be a woman who is in the position of a judge in a county or regional court who oversees child custody battles, and she regularly awards full custody of one or more children to the mother instead of the father.

In some instances, a man can very well exhibit the behavior of a *sexist* without automatically warranting the label of *misogynist*. Same with a woman. A woman can be very *sexist* toward men without necessarily warranting the label of a genuine *misandrist*.

There are many, many men and women in society who are *chauvinists* and/or *sexists* that do not literally "hate" members of the opposite sex. Then there are men who are *misogynists* and women who are *misandrists*.

In this chapter, I want to focus on women who are genuine *misandrists*, and even more specifically, what I like to refer to as ***Closet Misandrists***. There are some women, such as a few women who are

*Radical Feminists* who will never try to hide the fact that they are proponents of blatant misandry. Then, there are other women who exhibit misandry toward men in a more subtle and/or delayed manner. The latter group of women is who I generally refer to as ***Closet Misandrists***.

Quick clarification: Sometimes, a man can earn the label of *misandrist* just like a woman can earn the label of *misogynist*. Believe it or not, there are some men who **passionately hate other men** as an entire gender. For example, many men who fancy themselves as "male feminists" tend to fall into this category. Similarly, there are some women who **passionately hate other women**. For example, there are some women who hate other women who are *Radical Feminists*, or they hate other women who are "Pro-Choice" and heavily favor the legalization of abortion.

At minimum, a woman who is a genuine *misandrist* takes pleasure out of regularly belittling men, verbally emasculating men and disrespecting men, and publicly embarrassing and humiliating men. These women love forcing men to behave in a very submissive and subservient manner toward them.

At maximum, a woman who is a genuine *misandrist* has absolutely no desire to socially interact with men, no desire to date them, no desire to engage in sexual relations with them, and would prefer that all men be somehow lifted off the surface of Planet Earth to never be seen or heard from again.

Some men make the mistake of assuming that all women who are misandrists are women who publicly promote themselves as being *lesbians* and/or *Radical Feminists*. No, not true at all.

There are many women who are heterosexual or bisexual who operate as *Closet Misandrists*.

A *Closet Misandrist* is a woman who publicly wants to give men the impression that she does not really have a problem with men as a group, but deep down, she despises all men just based on their gender and genitalia.

The starting point for women who are *Closet Misandrists* is usually when they experience some type of physical and verbal abuse, sexual abuse and molestation, and/or sexual assault by one or more men as early as the age of 4, 5, or 6 or maybe as a pre-teen or teenager.

Or, it could be a scenario where the woman as a young child witnessed her mother, step-mother, or older sister being constantly mentally, emotionally, verbally, physically and sexually abused by some man who was a major presence in her life *(e.g., father, step-father, uncle, mother's boyfriend, etc.).*

At minimum, it will be a situation where the woman grows up feeling that the only thing men want from her is to use her body for their own sexual gratification and self-pleasure, or it could be that all of their former romantic companions and/or spouses cheated on them with other women.

Consequently, now this woman finds herself feeling extremely bitter and resentful toward just about the entire male gender. They then tend to maintain a long-lasting sense of disdain for the male gender as a whole.

Most of these women will usually make exceptions for men who are Gay, Bisexual, or very passive *Beta male* types who happen to be heterosexual.

The main challenge, or weakness, of women who are *Closet Misandrists* is that **a)** if they are a lesbian, they want to keep it a secret, and they want to publicly give off the impression of being heterosexual or **b)** if they are a heterosexual or bisexual *Radical Feminist*, they want to get pregnant by a man and they also want to gain the emotional and egotistical satisfaction of verbally emasculating their husband, fiancée, or long-term romantic companion for a number of years.

Sometimes, women who are *Closet Misandrists* will operate similar to that of a **Black Widow Spider**, meaning that once a man impregnates them, they will soon dismiss them *(not eat them or murder them, but just dismiss them. Some specific species of the Black Widow spider actually kill or even eat the male spiders who got them pregnant!)*.

Quick clarification: not ALL women who are lesbians and/or *Radical Feminists* are *misandrists* or *Closet Misandrists*. I want to make that clear. There are some lesbians who get along with men just fine, and there are even a small percentage of *Radical Feminists* who are very attracted to men and maintain long, healthy relationships and marriages with men.

A woman who is a lesbian is more likely to be an outspoken *misandrist* – if she has a genuine disdain for men – rather than choose to operate as a *Closet Misandrist*.

A woman who operates as a *Closet Misandrist* will usually be heterosexual, or at least, bisexual. Again, these women have a weakness for sexual reproduction with men (i.e., *procreation*).

A woman who is a *Radical Feminist* is simply a woman who is an advocate for women being treated equally in the workplace and equally in society, but they make the mistake of being very **extreme** with some of their beliefs, attitudes, and protests.

That extremism and radicalism is what separates them from more conventional feminists.

For example, a normal, conventional feminist believes that if men and women perform the exact same job with the exact same degree of skill and talent, then they should be paid an equal salary for that job. Similarly, a normal, conventional feminist will make every effort to ensure that girls can participate in organized sports (e.g., basketball) in the same way boys can.

On the other hand, a woman who is a *Radical Feminist* is a woman who might SAY that she is all about 'equality' between men and women, but in actual reality, this same woman ideally would like to see women **dominate** men and ultimately be in a position to influence every aspect of men's behavior and have women become the most influential thought leaders in society.

Personally, I have no problem with women who are lesbians *(that are not also misandrists)* and similarly, I have no problem with women who are conventional feminists *(that are not also misandrists)*. I have had women in both categories as co-workers and business colleagues before, and even a handful that have been close friends of mine.

On the other hand, I have no love or respect for women who are either outspoken misandrists or those who operate as *Closet Misandrists*. These women are the most guilty of **toxic femininity**.

The most extreme woman you will ever meet in your life is a woman who is a lesbian, a feminist *(and more specifically, a Radical Feminist)*, and an outspoken *misandrist* all wrapped up into one body.

These are the type of women that will be your most hardcore "man-haters." These are the women who completely despise men ... and want nothing to do with men ... and would never have sex with a man even if a man or woman had a gun to her head. These women could conceivably go on with the remainder of their lives without ever desiring to share the company of a man socially or otherwise.

Again, women who operate as *Closet Misandrists* are different.

Similar to the women I described in the very last chapter (Chapter Eight, when I discussed women who are *Drama Queens*, *Spoiled Divas*, and *Psycho Bitches*), these women know how to fool men into believing that they are innocent, easy-to-get-along-with, feminine and submissive companions in their early social interactions with men. They know how to 'play the role' of a woman who is anything BUT a genuine 'man-hater.'

Then, once you exchange wedding vows with this type of woman and/or this type of woman gives birth to the child that you impregnated her womb with, then this woman's disingenuous façade and her acting performance will come to an abrupt end. The highly successful "bait and switch" has been executed to perfection. Now, you will become her browbeaten and verbally emasculated victim.

From that day forward, the woman that is a certifiable *Closet Misandrist* will attempt to gain total control over each and every aspect of your marriage or long-term romantic relationship (LTR).

Some men who are active in *The Manosphere* will often maintain the invalid assumption that the vast majority of women want to date and ultimately marry men who are very dominant *Alpha male* types. Nothing could be further from the truth.

The women who I described in Chapter Six – the *Covert Gold Digger* types – have very little if any interest in dating or marrying a man who is a dominant and uncompromising *Alpha male* type. Will this type of woman engage in a one-night stand, a weekend fling, or some other variation of short-term and/or non-monogamous 'casual' sex with a man who is an *Alpha male* type? Sure.

When it comes to LTRs and marriage though, these women would prefer to date and marry a man who is a naïve, financially generous, easy-to-influence-and-manipulate *Beta male* type.

Same with many of the women who I described in Chapter Seven (the women who are *Ambitious Side Chicks* and *Man Thieves*). These women are more likely to target a naïve and/or financially generous *Beta male* type than they are to set their sights on a dominant and ultra-seductive *Alpha male* type. These women would be totally content with just engaging in some form of short-term and/or non-monogamous 'casual' sex with the men who are more *Alpha male* types.

And finally, the women who I described in Chapter Eight (the women who are *Drama Queens*, *Spoiled Divas*, and *Psycho Bitches*) most definitely would prefer to be in a LTR or marriage with a passive, easy-to-control-and-influence *Beta male* type than a truly dominant and financially cheap and stingy *Alpha male* type. Just like women who operate as *Covert Gold Diggers* and *Man Thieves*, these women would prefer to only engage in short-term and/or non-monogamous 'casual' sex with a man who is a true, genuine *Alpha male* type.

Contrary to popular belief, most true Alpha male types are **NOT** financially and materialistically generous with women. That is more of the M.O. of a man who I refer to as a *Beta Male with a Few Alpha Traits & Tendencies* (read my book titled, ***The Beta Male Revolution*** to find out more about this archetype of men as well as the other three archetypes of men). Some men in *The Manosphere* refer to financially generous *Beta Males with a Few Alpha Traits & Tendencies* as "High Value Men."

Weak, spineless *Beta male* types are most definitely the apple of the *Closet Misandrist*'s eye. *Closet Misandrists* literally prey on *Beta male* types. These women essentially operate like **predators** with men who are *Beta male* types.

I would say, even more specifically, women who operate as *Closet Misandrists* prey on men who are "fake" or disingenuous *Alpha male* types. In the same way there are many women who maintain *disingenuous façades* and *acting performances*, there are definitely men in society who do the **exact same thing**.

A woman who operates as a *Closet Misandrist* can quickly and easily detect "fabricated masculinity" in a man. If you are a man who deep down, is really a passive, lenient, overly accommodating, and easy-to-dominate *Beta male* type … but you are publicly

**pretending** to present yourself as a more dominant and full of masculine testosterone *Alpha male* type … then a woman who operates as a *Closet Misandrist* is going to **expose your disingenuous façade** at some point. She is going to **break you down**. Then, she is going to proceed to make you her personal *man-servant (i.e., bitch)* or *cuckold.*

The original formal definition of a *cuckold* is a man whose wife has repeatedly cheated on him with a number of men, but he is still willing to maintain the marriage or LTR with the unfaithful spouse or romantic companion. The second formal definition of a *cuckold* is a man who is married or romantically involved in a LTR, and his wife, fiancée, or long-term romantic companion allows another man to impregnate her … and instead of the man divorcing his wife or breaking up with his fiancée or long-term girlfriend, he decides to raise the son or daughter **that is not his** as if it were his own child. You would be surprised how many men in society have had a woman along with her designated male lover(s) leave them *cuckolded.*

In more modern and informal terms (especially if a man is part of the BDSM and/or Polyamory Lifestyle), a *cuckold* is a man who **voluntarily** and **enthusiastically** submits to his wife, fiancée, or long-term romantic companion, and gives her full authority to rule over him and 'wear the pants' in the relationship or marriage. He also allows her to openly invite other men to engage in sexual relations with her *(many times, while he watches her engage with her lovers like a lustful voyeur while he masturbates)*, and in some cases, he will allow his wife, fiancée, or long-term romantic companion to be impregnated by one or more other men (and he raises the child or children as his own).

I would venture to estimate that well over half of the women who have husbands and romantic companions who function as *cuckolds* are women who are either *Covert Gold Diggers*, *Drama Queens / Spoiled Divas / Psycho Bitches*, and/or *Closet Misandrists*.

Years ago, I remember watching this television crime drama where during one episode, the husband had to refer to his wife as "My Queen" and say to her "Yes, Ma'am" when responding to her demands and requests. In one scene, the husband says, *"Please, Ma'am. Please My Queen. I have been a good boy to you. A very obedient good boy to you. May I please have sex with you tonight My Queen?? Please?!?"*

I cringed listening to that man say that to his wife, even though it was just two fictional characters featured in a television drama. As you probably already surmised, I have issues with seeing a man begging his girlfriend, fiancée, or wife for sex or seeing a man become totally subservient to his wife, fiancée, or long-term romantic companion.

Over the years, I have known women who began a relationship with a male friend of mine, and initially, these women behaved in a manner that was very feminine, accommodating, and submissive.

Then, years later, after the woman and my friend had been married or romantically involved for a number of years, all of the sudden that same woman became very controlling, very dominant, and took every opportunity to verbally emasculate my male friend **in front of me**. A handful of my male friends admitted to me that they sometimes had to **beg** their wives or romantic companions for sex.

With one particular male friend of mine, once his long-term girlfriend gave birth to their daughter, she wanted nothing to do with him other than to collect child support payments from him. He later found out that his ex-girlfriend was bisexual, and in a romantic relationship with another woman.

Some Black men I know tend to assume that only Black women exhibit behavior that is masculine, controlling, and dominant. Yeah, RIGHT. In my adult life, I have observed such behavior from Asian women, Caucasian women, Middle Eastern women, and most definitely Hispanic women. Black women by no means have a monopoly on the concept of being a "Bossy Bitch" and/or a *Closet Misandrist*.

This is one of the reasons why many men in today's society are not too enthused about the concept of marriage, which is the basis for everything I discuss in my book titled ***The Beta Male Revolution***.

Among other things, men do not want to fall victim to a woman's "bait and switch" techniques, where they present themselves as one type of woman initially, but months or years later, the woman transforms into a totally different type of woman.

Any heterosexual man who considers himself to be a true, genuine *Alpha male* type would never allow himself to be repeatedly dominated and verbally emasculated by his wife, fiancée, or long-term girlfriend. He would rather remain single and unattached indefinitely than to put up with that B.S.

I don't care how beautiful or drop-dead gorgeous and sexy a woman is, or how much money she is earning from her lucrative career. If you are a true *Alpha male* type, you are not going to be subservient to the needs and wants of any woman.

Any man who is a true *Alpha male* type will immediately cease any social interaction with a woman who is not willing to adhere to **his program** (i.e., his terms & conditions for a LTR or marriage).

In contrast, if a man is a more passive and acquiescent *Beta male* type, he will temporarily or even indefinitely allow women (and sometimes, other men) to belittle him, disrespect him, humiliate him and generally emasculate him.

Once again, I have to emphasize that when you are in search of a woman to become your long-term girlfriend and potential fiancée and wife, you need to avoid all of the trivial *chit chat*, *fluff talk*, and *small talk* that many men choose to engage in with women of interest (reference Chapter Two).

You need to be engaging in **real, authentic conversations with a woman** so that you can identify **who this woman really is at her core**, and not buy into **who she is pretending to be**.

You need to ask this woman a lot of questions. Questions, questions, questions and even more questions. Take time to really get to know this woman in order to find out such things as **a)** how did her mother behave toward her father and vice versa? **b)** has she ever cheated on a man and/or had a man cheat on her? **c)** how is her relationship with her biological father? **d)** if she has one or more older brothers and/or one or more younger brothers, how is her relationship with them? **e)** who are her female role models who she seeks to emulate? **f)** how important is a man's looks, money and career success, fame, and social status to her?

It is easy for many women to maintain a disingenuous façade for a number of days, weeks, months, or even years, but if you indulge in real and authentic conversations with women from the beginning, you will essentially *force them* to reveal to you **who they really are**. Keep this in mind.

Always demonstrate how big your balls are and how firm and strong your backbone is to people and always carry yourself like **you are your own man**. Do not ever allow yourself to become a woman's *man-servant* (read: bitch) or her *cuckold* (unless that is a particular sexual *kink and fetish* of yours).

In my next chapter, which is the final chapter of this book, I am going to discuss women who you might think genuinely love you and adore you, and genuinely lust after you sexually, but in reality, these women are pathologically dishonest and are willing to cheat on you with other men (particularly, dominant and verbally seductive *Alpha male* types).

I refer to these women simply as ***Lustful & Cheating Liars***.

Continue reading my friend.

## Women to Avoid as Long-Term Romantic Companions #5: Lustful & Cheating Liars

Now, I have to give many of the heterosexual men who are about to read this fifth and final chapter of Part Two of this book a lighthearted "warning."

Within weeks after I first published my 2012 eBook edition of ***The Possibility of Sex*** as well as within weeks or months after I produced my 2014 audiobook edition of ***The Possibility of Sex***, I had dozens of men write me and convey to me that if there was at least one chapter in my book that left them feeling a bit angry, bitter, dejected, depressed, and just generally jaded and wary about the whole notion of long-term romantic relations with women (LTRs) and/or marriage, it was **this chapter**.

Just as recently as earlier this summer, I had a young man write me concerning this chapter. He said, *"Alan, I just got finished listening to your audiobook titled The Possibility of Sex, and man oh man. WOW.* ***That audiobook was a complete eye-opener for me, and particularly your very last chapter about women who are liars, cheaters, and adulterers****. WOW.* ***After listening to that chapter, I am now not sure if I will ever seek to get married****. I view women in a* ***totally different manner*** *after* *listening to your audiobook, and again, in particular, that very last chapter. WOW."*

Many men informed me that my book, ***The Possibility of Sex***, was literally the **very first book** they ever read (2012 eBook) or listened to (2014 audiobook) that explained *in detail* just how deceitful, duplicitous, manipulative, and scandalous many women in society can be with men.

Just a few weeks ago, on YouTube, I had a young African-American man by the name of Ramil who said during a livestream (slightly paraphrasing), *"I don't agree with everything Dating Coach Alan Roger Currie says in his book* ***Mode One****, and I haven't read his book* ***Oooooh ... Say it Again****, but just based on the knowledge and wisdom he provides to men in his two books* ***The Possibility of Sex*** *and* ***The Beta Male Revolution****, I would have to rank ARC as* ***the Greatest Dating Coach of All-Time!*** *Seriously man. Seriously. I believe just about every other dating coach and pickup artist in The Manosphere has been influenced and inspired over the last few years by those two books by ARC."*

If anyone was listening to that livestream that day on YouTube, they will remember that I actually broke down and **cried** momentarily in response to all of the flattering comments and praises that the young brother Ramil Amyr said about me and my books. I just really, really appreciated the love and respect he showed me that day. That was special.

Even though I am now married (as of mid-July 2020) and I now have a son, I totally empathize with and understand other men's reluctance to get married in the day and age we are living in now.

The blunt truth? There are just too many women in society today that are dishonest, disingenuous, sexually duplicitous and romantically unfaithful, and just highly manipulative and materialistic.

Take a few minutes to ponder over everything you read about the women I described in Chapter Six, Chapter Seven, Chapter Eight, and Chapter Nine. Marinate on everything thing I discussed.

Then, answer this simple question honestly: would you want to be in a LTR or marriage with any of those women who I described in those four chapters? I know for damn sure that I would not.

I have known my wife since April 2019, I have been dating her since June 2019, and as mentioned, I have been married to her since mid-July of this year. So far, so good. She has never displayed any signs of being a *Covert Gold Digger*, an *Ambitious Side Chick a.k.a. Man Thief*, a *Drama Queen / Spoiled Diva / Psycho Bitch*, and/or a *Closet Misandrist*. Fingers crossed for the future.

The final group of women I am going to discuss and describe under the category of "**toxic femininity**" are women who are ***Lustful & Cheating Liars***.

These are women who regularly, semi-regularly, or at least occasionally cheat on their husbands, fiancés, or long-term romantic companions, and 95-99% of the time, their spouses or male companions have absolutely **no clue or idea** that they are being cheated on. I mean, absolutely none.

I know this because beginning with the age of 17 all the way up until the age of 37, I was many women's "other man." Their "casual sex lover on-the-side" (or male "side piece").

Speaking of YouTube, once I became very active on YouTube beginning with April 2017, and I confessed this aspect of my personal life, a lot of men ended up harshly criticizing me for what I used to do. In one way or another, they said what I did was incredibly **disrespectful** to members of my own gender. And you know what? They are right.

This is why I stopped engaging in such behavior beginning with the age of 38, which would have been the calendar year 2001. At that time, I realized what I was doing was just plain wrong. As I alluded to in Chapter Six and Chapter Seven, I was 'enabling' women who are adulterous, disloyal and untrustworthy, and romantically unfaithful.

On one end, I am not at all proud of the number of women who I engaged in sexual relations with that were married at the time, engaged to be married at the time, or otherwise romantically involved with a long-term companion at the time.

But, the truth of the matter is – and I have mentioned this dozens of times before – a large part of my knowledge, wisdom, and keenly perceptive insight about women and their true **sexually duplicitous and romantically unfaithful nature** developed from this illicit sexual behavior that I experienced with other men's women.

The very first time I realized that women had a tendency to be sexually duplicitous and romantically unfaithful was probably my senior year in high school, which would have been the 1980-81 academic year.

Before my senior year in high school, I had always only received an average or even less-than-average degree of attention from girls. In middle school (sixth, seventh, and eighth grades), I was pretty much a semi-nerd, although I did participate in Pop Warner / CYO football.

I played football my freshman year in high school, but once I got demoted from playing the quarterback position by my coach because I was out of school for a few days with an illness, I lost interest in playing high school football. I quit the team the beginning of my sophomore year.

Then, I became obsessed with another sport ... **basketball**. I used to fantasize about becoming a *McDonald's All-American* high school basketball superstar, even though I had yet to play varsity or even junior varsity at my own high school.

I tried out for the team both my junior and senior year, and both times, I failed to make the final cut. I could shoot very well (I had a killer mid-range jumper!) and I had about a 28" or higher vertical leap (I had hops!) that I developed from wearing leg weights on my ankles for three years straight, but my 'handles' (i.e., dribbling skills) left a lot to be desired for someone my height (5'10" at the time).

Returning to the subject of getting attention from girls, the summer before my senior year, I worked out like crazy to prepare for basketball tryouts in the fall. I did wind sprints every other day, worked out with free weights every other day, and jogged 2 miles each and every day. I performed hundreds of push-ups each and every day.

The end result? Beginning with July 1980, I had a very lean, athletic, muscular physique. At that time, without question, it was the best physique I had ever possessed in my young life (I was 17 years of age).

So, even though I failed to make the basketball team (which was my dream), my "consolation prize" was that I received **a lot** of flattering attention from the girls in response to my newly developed physique.

What surprised me during my senior year was not just the attention I received from girls in general, but more specifically, how much flattering attention (and more specifically, sexual attention) I received from **girls who had long-term boyfriends**.

When I would attend many of my high school social events, a number of girls who were romantically involved in long-term relationships with other boys would literally sometimes just **throw themselves at me**. I mean, they would make it known that they wanted to make themselves available to me sexually if I desired to connect with them in a physically intimate manner.

You could say, in retrospect, what I experienced during my senior year in high school was the early stages for my first 'Red Pill' oriented enlightenment regarding the sexually duplicitous and romantically unfaithful nature of many women.

Toward the end of my senior year, I ended up engaging in sexual relations with the long-term girlfriend of one of my male classmates. A few weeks later, he found out.

He called me sounding a combination of **angry** and genuinely **hurt**. He said, *"Damn Al. How could you do this to me man? You fucked my girlfriend? Behind my back?? Man, that is so fucked up. I can't believe you would do that to me man."* Then, he just hung up the phone.

I felt bad about what had happened, but in my partial defense, I did not aggressively pursue his girlfriend. She aggressively pursued **me**. Pretty much each and every woman I engaged in short-term, non-monogamous 'casual' sex with during my senior year in high school made the first move on me. **They pursued me**. I rarely if ever pursued any of the girls I had sex with during my senior year.

If you already own my 1999 (eBook), 2006 (eBook and paperback), 2014 (audiobook) or 2017 (eBook) version of ***Mode One***, then you already know what was my second major instance of 'Red Pill' enlightenment regarding women.

It was when I viewed this adult film (porn flick) titled ***Talk Dirty to Me*** in summer 1981. I am not going to rehash and repeat everything about that movie that I already discussed in my various editions and versions of ***Mode One***, but in simple terms, it was that movie (and later, the sequel titled ***Talk Dirty to Me, Part II*** which I viewed in October of 1983) that first made me realize how sexually duplicitous and disingenuous women are.

To refresh your memory, when a man or woman is **sexually duplicitous**, this means that **publicly** they tend to present themselves as if they primarily or exclusively only engage in sexual relations with others within the context of a long-term, emotionally profound, strictly monogamous romantic relationship … but **privately**, behind closed doors … they will reveal a side to their personality and behavior that is kinkier and a bit more promiscuous and/or polyamorous.

For example, there are many women that when they are in the company of a man who they perceive to be a financially generous and/or more monogamy-oriented and family-oriented *Beta male* type, they will present themselves as the proverbial prudish or semi-prudish, strictly monogamy-oriented "**Good Girl**" type.

Conversely, when that **same woman** is in the company of a man who she views as a more smooth and seductive, highly masculine and dominant, and visually appealing *Alpha male* type, she will be more likely to be receptive to invitations to engage in some variation of short-term and/or non-monogamous 'casual' sex.

Real quick, go back and revisit everything I said on pages 80, 81, 82, and 83 related to my college days.

Remember when that woman who was a member of *Alpha Kappa Alpha, Inc. Sorority* said to me, *"Alan, I am going to be blunt honest with you. Us women?* ***We know the type of men that we want to engage in casual sex only with. We know. And those type of men are usually totally different than the type of men who we want as long-term boyfriends or husbands.*** *Just as I am sure that most of you men have different criteria for the women you want as your long-term companions or wives versus the women you want to be with for only a one-night stand or weekend fling."*

When it comes to the subject of women being *sexually duplicitous*, keep that quote from that woman in mind **forever**. She was telling **the truth**.

I don't want to spend too much in this chapter specifically discussing the sexually duplicitous nature of women, because I have already covered that subject in great detail in my book, ***Oooooh … Say it Again: Mastering the Fine Art of Verbal Seduction and Aural Sex***.

Real briefly though, I will say this: women, in a nutshell, do not view all men in the exact same manner (which, when you really think about it, is very similar to us men. Us men rarely view all women exactly the same).

I discussed this on some of my YouTube video podcasts in 2017, 2018, 2019, and I believe even earlier this year. Generally speaking, most men fall into one of four categories in the eyes of women:

1. Men who women will **only** engage in short-term and/or non-monogamous (casual) sex with. I usually refer to these men as *Total Alpha male* types;
2. Men who women **prefer** to be in a long-term, emotionally profound, romantic relationship with and ultimately marry (but many women may still '**settle**' for a few episodes of casual sex with these men). I usually refer to these men as an *Alpha male with a Few Beta Traits & Tendencies*;
3. Men who women will only engage in sex with, and particularly, short-term and/or non-monogamous sex with if they are being **financially compensated for it** by a man. I usually refer to these men as a *Beta male with a Few Alpha Traits & Tendencies*;

4. Men who women either **a)** only want to socially interact with in a non-physical, non-sexual, **purely platonic** manner, or **b)** do not want to socially interact with at all. I usually refer to these men as *Total Beta male* types.

When I was in my twenties and thirties, probably 4 out of every 5 women I engaged in sexual relations with had me in Category **#1** (casual sex only). I was 'Fuck Buddy' material for a lot of women, but rarely did women view me as long-term boyfriend and/or future fiancé and husband material.

The main factor that prevented me from falling into Category **#2** (boyfriend / husband material) or Category **#3** (Trick / Sugar Daddy / Financial Provider) was my lack of career success and financial success. Putting it more bluntly (as I already mentioned in Chapter Six on page 104), when I was between roughly 23 and 41, I was always either broke or financially struggling.

On the positive end, despite not having any wealth or material possessions to boast about, many women found me good looking to one degree or another, and even more so, many women found me to be *persuasively charming*, *verbally smooth and seductive*, and *kinky and dominant* in the bedroom.

Finally getting to the heart and main point of this chapter, I have had women over the years reveal to me who they **really were** ... particularly as it relates to **their true sexually duplicitous nature**.

Back in the 1960s, 1970s, 1980s, and to a lesser extent, the 1990s, the subject of "cheating" and "adultery" was almost always limited to **men**. In most television shows, movies, and magazine discussions, the question was always asked, "Why do MEN cheat so much?" Rarely did anyone ask, "Why do **women** cheat so much?"

Let me tell you this, assuming you do not know this already: **women are masterful cheaters and adulterers**. I mean, they are very, very, very good at it. As a group, women are far better cheaters and adulterers than the vast majority of men are. There are exceptions among both genders, but generally speaking ... based on my own experiences and observations ... women are much more meticulous and savvy with their cheating methods.

For example, do you know that some women will go as far as to introduce you to their husband, fiancé, or long-term boyfriend, and then proceed to engage in sexual relations with you behind their spouse or companion's back? In my adult life, I have had at least a half dozen women who did that.

It relates to the old adage of, "**The best way to hide something is to hide it in plain sight**."

Rarely if ever would a man do such a thing. Men would be very reluctant to introduce their mistress or side piece to their wife, fiancée, or long-term girlfriend, unless their mistress or side piece was already acquainted with their spouse or companion before they began cheating with them.

I once had a woman performing oral sex on me in the basement of her and her husband's house while her husband was upstairs preparing dinner for us. Believe it or not, I actually attempted to stop this woman from doing it, but she **insisted** on it.

Some women are just plain **scandalous** when it comes to cheating and adultery.

Why do so many of us in society have a bad habit of lying to people who are close to us? It could be a parent, a sibling, a child or another family relative, a spouse or romantic companion or anyone else we may interact with regularly or semi regularly.

There are a variety of reasons why men and women lie to members of their own gender as well as members of the opposite sex.

Based on my own experiences, here would be what I would categorize as the Top 5 reasons why many men and women will lie to their spouses or long-term romantic companions:

Reason **#1** for lying to your spouse or romantic companion: **so that you can be in a position to 'have your cake and eat it too'** Example: a woman who wants to enjoy the satisfying bedroom skills of a man who is broke and unemployed but wants to enjoy the financial and materialistic generosity of a man who is less-than-average in bed.

Reason **#2** for lying to your spouse or romantic companion: **to manipulate a situation in order to gain an opportunity to acquire the type of companionship that you would not be able to acquire if you were upfront and straightforwardly honest about your desires, interests and intentions** Example: a man is reluctant to openly express a desire to be polyamorous and regularly engage in non-monogamous sex with multiple women because he knows that 99.9% chance, his beautiful and sexy wife would divorce him if she found out he wasn't as monogamy-oriented as she originally assumed.

Reason **#3** for lying to your spouse or romantic companion: **to prevent yourself from being criticized and admonished, and/or to prevent yourself from experiencing consequences and repercussions that you would rather avoid**

Example: a woman hides or lies about her highly promiscuous past to prevent her fiancé from developing 'second thoughts' about marrying her and ultimately calling off the wedding.

Reason #4 for lying to your spouse or romantic companion: **to give your spouse or romantic companion the misleading impression that you are one type of person, when in actuality, you are a totally different type of person** Example: a man misleads his long-term girlfriend into believing that he is way more religious and spiritual than he really is in order to motivate his deeply religious girlfriend to remain with him indefinitely.

Reason #5 for lying to your spouse or romantic companion: **to avoid bruising the ego and/or hurting the feelings of your spouse or romantic companion** Example: a woman who lies to her husband and tells him that he is "great in bed," even though in reality, she feels that his bedroom skills are boring, disappointing, and unsatisfying.

Did you know that most surveys show that **honesty** and **loyalty** are the **top qualities** that most men want in a wife, fiancée, or long-term romantic companion?

For most men, **honesty**, **loyalty**, and overall **trustworthiness** rank much higher in importance than a woman's physical appearance and level of attractiveness, her degree of sex appeal, her degree of intelligence and formal education, her sense of humor and wit, or even her maternal instincts.

Many men feel that if a woman does not possess a high degree of honesty, loyalty, and overall trustworthiness, then there is no point of even entering into a long term relationship or a marriage with that particular woman. If a woman does not possess these highly desired traits, she will usually be relegated to being nothing more than a casual sex lover (Fuck Buddy) for most men.

I remember back in 2012, I was once interviewed on this national talk radio show along with two licensed psychologists, both women, and one other male guest who had some type of formal academic credentials in the area of Relationship Psychology and/or Marriage and Family Therapy.

The subject of this particular episode of the nationally syndicated talk radio program was *Why Do Women Cheat and Commit Adultery?*

Throughout the course of the talk radio discussion, all of the other three guests kept offering comments such as, *"Well, when men cheat, it is usually strictly because they cannot control their sexual urges while in the company of a beautiful and sexy woman, but when women cheat and commit adultery, it is usually because their boyfriend or husband is ignoring them and not paying them enough attention, which causes an emotional void for the woman. Blah, blah, blah, blah, blah . . ."*

Just about all of the comments of the other three guests generally **defended women** who cheated, but **harshly admonished men** who cheated.

I was the only guest on this talk radio program, out of the four guests who were being interviewed, who was bold enough to say that women cheat on men for many of the same reasons that men cheat on women, which is most prominently **exciting, kinky, and orgasmically satisfying sex**.

For the vast majority of women, that whole notion of cheating because of an 'emotional void' is total B.S. I have never had a woman choose me as her "other man" or "casual sex lover on-the-side" in order to fill any sort of "emotional void." The women who chose me just wanted some *good dick.*

I have even heard many men in *The Manosphere* perpetuate this invalid notion that "women are far more emotional than men are, therefore, if you want to get women in bed, you have to appeal to their emotional side ..." I am here to tell you: **THAT IS STRAIGHT UP BULLSHIT.**

When I was between the age of 17 and 37, I engaged in sexual relations with no less than 35 women who happened to be married at the time, engaged to be married at the time, or otherwise romantically involved with a long-term boyfriend.

Out of those roughly 35-40 women, I would estimate that only about 6 or 7 of them found themselves becoming "emotionally attached" to me after a number of episodes of our kinky sex.

The other women never once hinted to me that they had become 'emotionally attached' to me or that they wanted to fill some sort of 'emotional void.'

Generally speaking, the only time women tend to become emotionally attached to a man is when he spends a significant amount of quality time with those women both sexually **AND** non-sexually.

This is one of the reasons why when I deal with women for short-term non-monogamous casual sex, I never like to "blur the lines" between treating a woman like a *Fuck Buddy* only and treating her like a potential long-term girlfriend or future wife.

I know many, many men who have made this mistake, including close friends of mine, fraternity brothers of mine, and even a couple of male relatives of mine.

I remember when even one of own male cousins once said to me, *"Cuz, I like some aspects of your Mode One Approach, but the one thing I am not down with is that it seems that when you have a woman you're dealing with just for casual sex, you treat her like she is nothing more than a Fuck Buddy."* I was like, "And? Your point is … ?"

He went on to say, *"I can't do that. That would make me feel like I am being some sort of 'jerk' or 'asshole' to the woman.* ***I always want a woman to feel like she at least has a chance to someday become my long-term girlfriend or future wife*** *..."*

What my cousin was basically endorsing was using **dishonesty and psychological & emotional manipulation** to get women in bed. Most dating coaches and PUAs who teach various forms of **indirect** (verbal) **game** emphasize this and endorse it and condone it to their clients and followers.

As most of you already know, I let women know **upfront** and **straightforwardly** that all I desire to do is engage in one or more episodes of short-term and/or non-monogamous 'casual' sex with them. I do not toy with women's emotions or lead them on. I despise men who are **blatant liars** and **seek to manipulate women psychologically and emotionally** just for a few episodes of short-term casual sex.

The blunt honest truth is that women love to fuck just like men love to fuck. In the same way most men view some women as "casual sex only" material while they view other women as "potential long-term girlfriend or wife" material, many women have those **exact same delineations**.

When it comes to casual sex lovers, women prefer men who are very confident, very masculine, very verbally smooth and seductive, kinky and erotically dominant, and of course, satisfying in bed.

Next to being satisfying in bed, I would say the most important two qualities that most helped me get women in bed was my **verbal seduction skills** and **erotic dirty talk talents** and my **supreme level of confidence** and **erotic dominance** with women.

This once again highlights the appeal of *Alpha male* types versus *Beta male* types. *Alpha male* types are the men who turn women on more sexually, and *Beta male* types are the men who women find more appealing as far as their **non-sexual** attention and companionship as well as their **financial and materialistic generosity**.

I was never "romantic" with any of the women I engaged in sexual relations with that were married, engaged to be married, or had a long-term boyfriend. I was **verbally kinky** and **extremely**

**dominant** with these women, Much more so than their husbands, their fiancés, or their boyfriends.

Women can fill an 'emotional void' with a good extracurricular hobby, such as crochet lessons, bowling, or ballroom dancing, or they can fill an 'emotional void' with the companionship of a number of purely platonic male friends.

Fact: Women cheat on men when they are *satisfied* with their spouse or long-term companion's **non-sexual attention and companion**, but they are *dissatisfied* with his **bedroom skills and prowess**.

In other words, if your wife, fiancée, or long-term girlfriend ever becomes dissatisfied with the **non-sexual component** of your marriage or LTR, she is not going to cheat on you indefinitely. No Sir. She is ultimately going to **leave you**.

Women rarely divorce men or break up with men because of sexual dissatisfaction only. Occasionally? Maybe. In general though, if you are a man who is taking care of all of a woman's **non-sexual** wants and needs and all of her **financial and materialistic** wants and needs, there is a 99% chance that this woman is going to stay with you even if the sex is disappointing or unsatisfying.

If the only thing missing in her long-term relationship with you or her marriage with you is sexual satisfaction, then that woman will simply resort to cheating on you with one or more verbally smooth & seductive, kinky, masculine, and sexually dominant *Alpha male* types behind your back.

One story I have repeated dozens of times is one involving a very beautiful and sexy Caucasian Blonde I used to fuck back in 1995 when I lived in Los Angeles. This woman would probably rank as an "8.5" or even a "9" on most men's "1" to "10" scale of female beauty and feminine sex appeal.

The first two times she and I had sex, I never saw a wedding ring on an engagement ring on her finger. Then, the third time we had sex, I see this HUGE diamond ring on her finger. I was like, "You're married?!?" She responded, *"No. I am engaged."*

Turns out, her fiancé was some sort of computer software engineer and entrepreneur who at the time, was earning close to a million dollars per year. She was driving a *Porsche 911* that her fiancé had purchased for her.

This woman ended up telling me that not only was her fiancé unsatisfying sexually, but that she did not even enjoy engaging in sex with Caucasian men.

I was like, "What??? Are you serious??" She said, *"Very. Sexually, I much prefer being with Black men, but I would never, ever marry a Black man."*

I then asked her a "dumb" question. I said, "If your fiancé doesn't do it for you in bed, then why in the hell are you marrying him?" She just lightheartedly frowned at me and shook her head. That was the somewhat "naïve" version of Alan Roger Currie asking her that ridiculously silly question.

Her fiancé was formally educated (I believe Stanford MBA), he grew up in an upper-middle-class family, and he was affluent with a high degree of career success.

Her attitude was, "When a man is rich, educated, and has a high degree of social status and career success, you don't break up with a guy like that. You simply cheat on him whenever you can."

So, for all those men who believe money is the #1 thing that leads to **casual sex success** with women … WRONG. I never spent $5.00 on that woman, yet I used to fuck her whenever I wanted to. I never treated her to lunch, I never treated her to dinner, or even took her to a movie for free.

And again, this woman was **gorgeous**. She was what young men today refer to as a *P.A.W.G.* (i.e., a Caucasian woman with a small waist, but a big, round, juicy butt).

Many highly manipulative and materialistic women and sexually duplicitous women in society want you to naively believe that they are not quite as interested in sexual enjoyment and satisfaction in the same manner that the vast majority of men are.

**This is how they 'run game' on naïve and lustful men.** Particularly, *Beta male* types. Manipulative women, materialistic women, and sexually duplicitous women never, ever want to engage in short-term or long-term sex with a *Beta male* type for **FREE**. If that man is not offering them something of monetary or tangible value, then he can forget about having sex with these types of women. It is simply not going to happen.

The only men that the women I described in Chapter Six, Chapter Seven, Chapter Eight, and to a far lesser extent, Chapter Nine want to engage in short-term and/or non-monogamous sex with without those men spending money on them or committing to them long-term are verbally smooth & seductive, kinky and dominant *Alpha male* types.

If the only two ways you are able to engage in sexual relations with a woman is either by **a)** spending a lot of money on her and 'Wining & Dining' her and/or **b)** promising her long-term strict monogamy, then that means you are a *Beta male with a Few Alpha Traits and Tendencies* (or again, what some men in *The Manosphere* now refer to as a "High Value Man").

When you are a true womanizing *Alpha male* type, you do not have to spend money on women to get them in bed, nor do you have to promise them any sort of long-term commitment to get them in bed. **Especially** if we are talking about women who are already married, engaged to be married, or already have a long-term romantic companion.

There are approximately 2 to 3 times more **nerve endings** in a woman's **clitoris** (approximately 7,500 - 8,000) than there are nerve endings in the **head of a man's penis** (approximately 2,500 - 3000).

What this means is, when you stimulate a woman's clitoris and bring her to orgasm, she is experiencing two to three times more joy, excitement and sexual satisfaction than you are as a man *(which is why women usually **moan so loud** if the sex is very enjoyable to them)*. Think about that for a moment.

Never allow yourself to buy into the misguided notion that all men are significantly hornier than all women. At least half of the reason why many women choose to **pretend** as though they are not into sex as much as men is because they know by doing so they can take advantage of men who are naïve, sexually desperate, and financially generous.

Think about it: if all heterosexual and bisexual women in the world came out and announced that they were just as horny if not hornier for sex as men are, would you as a man be motivated to …

A) **Spend hours on top of hours flattering them**? (FYI: re-read Chapter One)

B) **Entertaining them** and **engaging in lengthy and trivial, but highly entertaining** ***chit chat*****,** ***fluff talk*****, and** ***small talk?*** (FYI: re-read Chapter Two)

C) **Offering them free meals, expensive materialistic gifts, and other monetary favors before you even engaged in sexual relations with them for the first time?** (FYI: re-read Chapter Three)

D) **Pretending indefinitely to be content with remaining a woman's purely platonic male friend when you know you want more?** (FYI: re-read Chapter Four)

E) **Feeling that you have to resort to lying to women, misleading and manipulating women, or worse, date-raping women?** (FYI: re-read Chapter Five)

All men know the answer to all five questions. It is NO. Realistically, more so **HELL NO**.

Get real fellas. Just about every type of *manipulative head game* that a woman is able to execute with a man starts with her being able to persuade you to believe that her sexual companionship is far more desirable and valuable to YOU than yours is to HER.

I would be willing to guarantee you, that if from this day forward, you were to begin treating each and every woman you meet as if she were just as horny for your sexual companionship as you were for hers, your whole attitude and demeanor & disposition toward women would slowly but surely **change**.

When I interact with women, I never behave as if I am five times more horny for sex than they are. Never. I always treat women with a very cocky attitude that they desire my sexual companionship just as much **if not more** than I desire theirs.

Sadly, for some women, even a LTR or marriage is nothing more than one prolonged version of a tactical *manipulative head game* with a male target.

Do you honestly believe that **every woman** who currently has a long-term boyfriend genuinely loves him, and has never, ever cheated on him and never would cheat on him in the future? GET REAL.

Do you honestly believe that **every woman** who is currently engaged to be married genuinely loves her fiancé, and has never, ever cheated on him and never would cheat on him in the future if given the opportunity to do so? GET REAL.

Do you honestly believe that **every woman** who is currently married is genuinely in love with their husband and has never, ever cheated on him and never would cheat on him in the future if given an opportunity to do so? GET REAL.

Most of the women who are going to cheat on their husband, fiancé, or long-term romantic companion are the women who I discussed and described in my previous chapters.

For example, *Covert Gold Digger* types will almost always cheat on men. If you end up marrying or getting into a LTR with a woman who used to be your mistress or side piece *(i.e., the Ambitious Side Chick a.k.a. Man Thief)*, nine times out of ten, she is going to cheat you. *Drama Queens* and *Spoiled Divas* are usually going to cheat on men *(unless they transition into becoming more of a Psycho Bitch and kill the man first)*. Even *Closet Misandrists* will probably cheat on a few men, but if they do, it will probably be with another woman more so than with another man.

I remember once watching this episode of *Dr. Phil.* There was this couple on Dr. Phil's afternoon TV talk show named Kim and Cliff. The couple had recently entered into a form of polyamory known as *couple swapping*. The problem was Cliff wanted to have sex with his wife, Kim, but she admitted on national television that she found her husband totally unappealing physically and sexually, and totally unsatisfying in bed.

I found myself feeling sorry for Cliff because he was being humiliated by his wife in front of a national television audience. I could tell that even Dr. Phil felt sorry for Cliff, but at the same time, Dr. Phil was amazed that Cliff had yet to file for divorce from his wife Kim.

At one point, Dr. Phil asked Kim why she chose to remain with Cliff if she did not find him sexually appealing or satisfying in bed. To no surprise to me, Kim began emphasizing all of his **non-sexual** attributes, characteristics, and redeeming qualities.

I say again: if a woman feels as though her husband, fiancé, or long-term boyfriend is fully satisfying all of her **non-sexual** wants and needs and all of her **financial & materialistic** wants and needs, then 99% chance she is never going to divorce that man or break up with that man simply because of disappointing and unsatisfying sex. She is going to simply resort to cheating on him with men who are more sexually appealing and more satisfying in bed. Either regularly, semi-regularly, or at minimum, occasionally.

At least I give the woman Kim props for not cheating on Cliff behind his back. Instead, she persuaded him to convert their former strictly monogamous marriage into a more open and polyamorous marriage.

At the risk of generalizing, men who have never had even one woman *cheat on them* and/or *cheat with them* are typically going to be your most naïve, 'Blue Pill' type men.

Just about all of the men I have ever known that maintained the most keenly perceptive insight on women's true sexually duplicitous and romantically unfaithful nature were men, like myself, who had been a number of women's "other man" or "casual sex lover on-the-side."

I gained so many nuggets of wisdom and insight by being many women's 'other man,' and that is why I don't totally regret my sexual experiences with those women who happened to be married, engaged to be married, or otherwise romantically involved.

If I had never had those experiences, nine times out of ten, I would've never developed the knowledge and wisdom it takes to be a top-notch dating coach.

What's funny is, I am typically more known for my book, ***Mode One***, but it is this book … ***The Possibility of Sex*** … that has arguably earned me the most praise and respect from men under the category of "waking them up" so that they could realize just how sexually duplicitous and romantically unfaithful women can be, as well as how highly manipulative and extremely materialistic many women can be.

Did you know I once read an article that pointed out that women are three times more likely than men to have an extramarital affair with someone who is a sibling, relative, close friend, or business colleague of their spouse or long-term romantic companion? On the other hand, when men cheat, they usually cheat with a woman who is not acquainted with their wife, fiancée, or long-term girlfriend.

Yep, some women are that damn scandalous. If you ever happen to notice that one of your male friends or business colleagues is starting to become way too familiar with your wife, fiancée, or long-term girlfriend, and you are noticing that he is almost flirting with her, if only in a very subtle manner, you might want to step in and nip that shit in the bud with a quickness.

I have heard some dating and relationship experts (particular those who are women) suggest that you should never, ever ask a woman about her sexual past. **Bullshit.** I always do. Now if you are interacting with a woman who is nothing more than a casual sex lover (Fuck Buddy), then there is no point in asking a woman about her sexual past. Who cares.

But if you are interacting with a woman who you view as a potential long-term girlfriend and possibly a future fiancée and wife, then ask questions. Ask a hell of a lot of questions. Even questions that may leave a woman feeling a bit uneasy and uncomfortable. Again, this is how you provoke a woman to show you **who she really is** as opposed to **who she may be pretending to be**.

Even if she happens to lie to you about some aspects of her past, at least you asked. She can never say to you, "Well, you never asked." I remember a male friend asking his ex-girlfriend, *"Why didn't you ever tell me that you were bisexual and into having sex with other women??"* She responded, *"You never asked."*

I realize that a lot of women do not like to be asked questions about their past relationships or their sexual past in general, but my attitude is, if this is a woman that you are contemplating spending **the rest of your adult life with** and possibly raising children with, you need to find out as much as possible about the character and quality of woman you are currently dealing with. You do not want to experience any major regrets down the line.

If you are constantly catching a woman you are currently dating in lie after lie after lie, **cut her ass loose**. That is an untrustworthy woman. Lies always come back to bite a person in the butt in the long-run. Men and women who are ***Lustful & Cheating Liars*** always get exposed in the long-run.

You can usually sense that a woman is cheating on you when you have to damn near 'beg' your wife, fiancée, or long-term romantic companion to engage in sex with you.

If you are married or in a LTR, are you the one that always has to initiate sex? Or does your wife, fiancée, or long-term romantic companion sometimes initiate sex with you?

In just about every LTR I have ever been involved with, I never had to resort to begging a woman for sex. No less than two-thirds of the time, my ex-girlfriends and former lovers would **initiate** sex.

When I speak with men who are suspicious that their spouse or romantic companion is cheating on them behind their back, I have noticed that a lot of these men are overly concerned about their penis size. They want to know if their significant other is cheating on them specifically because their penis is not long enough and/or not thick enough.

Let me be real. Penis size is important to a degree, but the length and/or girth of your penis is not **everything** to all women. The two types of men who will usually have the most problems with women as far as the size of their penis is usually going to be those men who are on one extreme or the other (i.e., women consider your penis to be either *way too small* or *way too big*).

Do you know that on at least three different occasions, I engaged in sex with a woman who was a *Lustful & Cheating Liar* that informed me that their husband, fiancée, or boyfriend had a penis that was either longer than mine and/or thicker than mine. The first time was when I was 24 years old. I was having sex with this (Black) woman who was cohabiting with her boyfriend.

She once showed me a photo of her boyfriend. Her boyfriend was much taller than me. That mildly surprised me, because there has always been this belief that women (and particularly Black women) prefer taller men. I am just under 5'11", and this woman's boyfriend was about 6'3" or 6'4".

While we were having sex once, I was lightheartedly bragging about the size of my dick. That is when she said, *"With all due respect Alan, my boyfriend's dick is bigger than yours. It is longer and slightly thicker too."* I lightheartedly feigned as if I were angry by responding to her, "What in the hell?!?!? Then why in the hell are you cheating on him with me!!!" I wasn't really angry or upset, but my ego was a tad bit bruised.

She basically went on to tell me that even though her boyfriend's dick was bigger than mine, she enjoyed having sex with me more because she said I was **a)** more **verbally kinky** than her boyfriend and **b)** more **erotically dominant** than her boyfriend.

She described her boyfriend as more of a passive, verbally prudish 'nice guy' type, and she generally described him as more of a *Beta male* type personality and behavior wise, although physically, he looked like more of an *Alpha male* type.

This brings me to something I mentioned when I spoke at this event in 2018 titled *The 21 Convention* in Orlando, Florida. Many men who are active in *The Manosphere* are familiar with this event.

I mentioned in my speaking presentation that a lot of men seem to label men as being "Alpha" on certain criteria that is not always 100% valid.

Three examples would be **1)** men who are tall, **2)** men who have a very muscular physique, and **3)** men who are wealthy or successful entrepreneurs.

A man does not necessarily need any of those three attributes to be viewed as an *Alpha male* type in the eyes of most women, and especially criteria #3 (wealth and career success).

Wealth and career success have very little if anything to do with a woman viewing you as a womanizing *Alpha male* type. Nothing. If anything, I would classify career success, financial success, and financial and materialistic generosity as more of a *Beta male* trait.

As I have already mentioned in this book, when I was a prolific womanizer between the age of 21 and my early-to-mid forties, I rarely if ever spent any money on women before I engaged in sexual relations with them for the first time. Most of the time, **the women spent more money on me than I ever spent on them**. The truth is, I never had any money or materialistic gifts to offer women when I was in my twenties and thirties. I was usually struggling financially.

True *Alpha male* types almost always pull women on a combination of **a)** their physical appearance, **b)** their degree of confidence and their masculine demeanor and disposition *(otherwise known as their 'masculine sex appeal')*, and **c)** their persuasive and seductive charm and overall conversation skills *(otherwise known as a man's 'mouthpiece')*.

In relation to criteria #1 (height) and #2 (muscularity), a man does not necessarily have to be tall and/or possess an exceptionally muscular physique in order for a woman to view him as an *Alpha male* type.

Now, don't get me wrong … being tall and/or muscular will definitely not "hurt" your chances of being successful with women, but neither attribute is an absolute "mandatory requirement" for being considered *Alpha* in the eyes of women.

I have known many men in my life who were taller than me and/or possessed a more muscular physique than me that were not more verbally smooth and seductive than me with women, and not more verbally kinky or more erotically dominant than me with women.

In other words, it is very conceivable that a man can be tall and/or muscular, and still have the **personality** and **behavior patterns** of a *Beta male* type. I actually have had some dating coaching clients over the last few years who fit this description.

In my opinion, you can never become a **master seducer** of women without a powerful and persuasive *mouthpiece*. It is virtually impossible.

The reason being is that **seduction is pretty much all verbal**. There is really no such thing as a "non-verbal seduction."

Any man who is able to engage in sexual relations with multiple women without possessing a powerful and persuasive mouthpiece is not actually seducing those women. Those women are just responding to the visual and aesthetic appeal of his face and/or physique. That is **not seduction**. That is **attraction**. Reference Chapter Three, pages 55-60.

A man cannot get a woman who is a *Wholesome Pretender* or an *Erotic Hypocrite* in bed with just looks alone. Women who are *Reciprocators*? Sure. Women who are *Reciprocators* tend to respond favorably to men just based on the man's face, physique, and demeanor & disposition alone.

On the other hand, when a woman is either a *Wholesome Pretender* type and/or an *Erotic Hypocrite* type, then a man is going to have to possess some degree of verbal seduction skills, erotic dirty talk talents, and persuasive charm.

**Verbal Seduction** and **Erotic Dirty Talk** is the primary subject that I discuss in my book, ***Oooooh … Say it Again*** along with the *sexually duplicitous nature of women* in general.

One **non-physical attribute** that will lead to many women often getting bored with you and ultimately cheating on you is if you're simply "too nice." This means, you're way too non-confrontational and too pleasant, lenient, accommodating, and financially generous. Your behavior is just way too predictable.

Women prefer men who have some sort of 'edge' about them. One thing that always gave me an 'edge' with women when I was younger was the fact that I was super COCKY with women, despite the fact that I had a low degree of career success and financial success. I would talk to women with an attitude of, *"I KNOW you want to share my company. I KNOW you do ..."*

In addition to being boring, some men have weight problems or grooming and personal hygiene issues. If you fall into this category, take the necessary steps to correct this. Make sure you eat right, exercise, dress well and bathe or shower regularly.

Also, some men are just "lazy lovers." I have known women to complain about their husband, fiancé, or boyfriend being a "lazy lover." What that means is, she actually enjoys her man's sexual companionship, but her man does not seem to be as interested in having sex with her as frequently as she is interested in having sex with him.

This happens quite a bit when a man is cheating on his wife, fiancée, or long-term romantic companion with one or more other women.

Some men get cheated on as *revenge* for their wife, fiancée, or long-term girlfriend finding out that her husband, fiancé, or long-term boyfriend was cheating on her **first**.

Again, I despise men and women who blatantly lie to their spouses and romantic companions, and cheat on them behind their back. Even though I have engaged in sexual relations with a number of women who were *Lustful & Cheating Liars*, I have not cheated on a companion of mine behind her back since I was like 20 or 21 years old.

Beginning with the age of 22 until my current age, I always let women know that I do not believe in "strict" and/or "obligatory" long-term monogamy. In other words, I will remain monogamous to a woman as long as my desire to do so is genuine, enthusiastic, and voluntary, but the moment I feel like I am only being faithfully monogamous to a woman because I feel pressured to be, then I am done being faithfully monogamous with women.

Many of the long-term romantic relationships in my adult life have been ***polyamorous***. A polyamorous relationship is when your relationship with a woman is long-term and involves some degree of an emotional attachment, but there is no 'strict' and/or 'obligatory' sense of monogamy involved. If there is a long stretch where you happen to be monogamous with your spouse or partner, it is because you CHOOSE TO BE faithfully monogamous … and not because you feel as though you HAVE TO BE faithfully monogamous.

A woman's honesty is more important to me than her romantic or sexual faithfulness. Any man who fancies themself as being 'Red Pill' knows that women are ultimately going to do whatever it is they really, really want to do. So, if they really want to fuck a man other than their husband, fiancé, or long-term boyfriend, **they are going to do it**.

If any spouse or romantic companion of mine were to engage in sexual relations with another man without asking my permission first, or without openly informing me about her intentions to do so ahead of time, then that marriage or long-term relationship would end immediately. I don't tolerate dishonesty or sneaky, behind-my-back behavior.

In closing, I very much hope that these last five chapters in Part Two of this updated edition of ***The Possibility of Sex*** has provided you with some food for thought if you happen to be married, engaged to be married, romantically involved with a woman long-term, or may be searching for your next long-term girlfriend or future fiancée and wife.

Many men have told me that I have functioned as the father they never had or the big brother they never had, and I more than appreciate those types of compliments from my (male) followers, supporters, and clients.

A lot has changed for me in my personal life since I wrote and published the first edition of this book back in fall 2012. I am now happily married and as of the publishing date of this book, I have a 3-month old son named Cayden.

I remember when one of my uncles told me many years ago, *"Son, marriage is either going to be the closest thing to Heaven on Earth ... or the closest thing to Hell on Earth ... depending on **the quality of woman** you choose to marry. Choose the right quality of woman, you will be in Heaven. Choose the wrong type of woman, you will be in Hell."*

I cannot predict what the future holds for me as far as my marriage with my wife goes, but so far, I am in **Heaven**. Marriage suits me just fine at my age.

I thoroughly enjoy being a book author, a freelance writer, an audio and video podcaster, and a professional dating coach.

I have a passionate and empathetic interest in helping my male clients clarify things about interacting with women that they do not yet understand, helping them experience epiphanies that they had never experienced previously, and generally assisting them in improving their **verbal communication skills** with women of interest.

The single biggest takeaway from this book for men is to always exhibit behavior that is **real** and **authentic** with women of interest.

Do not give in to the temptation of being a blatant liar with women, a man who psychologically and emotionally manipulates women, and/or a man who is simply a verbal coward or hateful misogynist.

Remember: the more you go out of your way to attempt to 'run game' on women, the more you automatically open yourself up to have savvy, seasoned *Manipulative Timewaster* types and the other assorted types of women that I have described in the various chapters of this book 'run game' on **YOU**.

Thank you for taking the time to read this revised and updated version of ***The Possibility of Sex*** in its entirety. I hope you have learned from it.

Enjoy your life my friend.

# Wrap Up & Closing Thoughts

On the surface, this book is going to be perceived by readers (and particularly, female readers) as a book that is designed to exclusively target, criticize, and expose all of the most unappealing and undesirable behavioral traits of heterosexual and bisexual women.

To a degree, that assessment is fairly valid, but exposing women's manipulative and materialistic tendencies as well as the flaws and weaknesses of their moral character and integrity was more so the #2 priority of this book.

The #1 priority of this book was to emphasize to men that when they employ a style of **verbal communication** with women that is **dishonest**, **disingenuous**, **misleading and manipulative**, and/or **overly cautious** and **cowardly**, they will very frequently place themselves in a position for manipulative women with self-serving objectives to exploit them and take advantage of everything tangible and intangible they have to offer.

If there is one discussion and debate I have always found myself drawn into is one regarding other dating coaches and pickup artist types (PUAs) presenting the argument that **indirect** verbal communication with women is less risky and more socially acceptable than **verbally bold** and **direct** verbal communication.

Of course, any variation of indirect verbal communication is going to be deemed as more socially appropriate than being verbally bold and direct, because when you exhibit some variation of **indirect** (verbal) **game**, you are not exhibiting any real **BALLS** or **BACKBONE** with women.

At minimum, when you employ indirect verbal communication styles with women, you are being what is known as a *social conformist.* At maximum, your indirect behavior is representative of being a **blatant liar**, a **disingenuous and misleading manipulator**, and/or a **verbal coward**.

All of the behavior that I described in the first four chapters of this book is the direct result of **a man being profoundly afraid of being abruptly or straightforwardly rejected by a woman** of interest, and also **a man being afraid of women harshly criticizing him, insulting him, or displaying some sort of negative reaction to something he said, or the manner in which he said it**.

I am not afraid of either response. I love it when women reject me sooner rather than later. I would rather a woman reject my romantic advances or strictly sexual advances within the first five-to-ten minutes of my very first conversation and social interaction with her, then to have a woman join me for two or three dinner dates, only to let me know that she has no interest in sharing my company in a physically intimate manner by the end of the second date.

Particularly if we are referring to some variation of short-term and/or non-monogamous 'casual' sex. It does not take women hours, days, weeks, or months to decide if they are going to engage in *casual sex* with a man. Generally speaking, **women know within 15 minutes or less** after they first meet you if you are the type of man who they would engage in some form of short-term and/or non-monogamous sexual relations with without any sort of emotional attachment or monogamous commitment being involved.

If you enjoyed this book, please recommend it and refer it to your friends. I would very much appreciate that gesture. Also, please post a review and rating on Amazon.com within a few days after you have finished reading the book. I would surely appreciate it.

If you did not enjoy this book (man or woman), I invite you to write me and share with me in a very specific, intelligent, and objective manner what portion of this book you had philosophical disagreements with. I would be interested in reading your comments and objective criticisms.

**Women** ... quit trying to take advantage of naïve, horny, and/or wealthy men. One day, you are going to engage in manipulative 'head games' with the wrong type of man *(one that is mentally and emotionally unstable and/or physically violent)*, and you are going to suffer some very unpleasant consequences. In the same manner that the vast majority of women do not like to have their emotions toyed with, neither do most men. If you are not genuinely interested in sharing a man's company in a romantic or strictly sexual manner, let him know that **by the end of your very first face-to-face conversation** (and no later than your second face-to-face conversation) **with him**.

**Men** … if your specific objective is to engage in one or more episodes of short-term and/or mon-monogamous 'casual' sex with a woman, then have the **BALLS** and **BACKBONE** to verbally communicate those desires and interests to her in a confident, highly self-assured, upfront, specific, and straightforwardly honest manner. This is what I have done for literally **36 years**.

*Mode One Baby ... Quit being afraid of rejection and negative reactions and responses from women.*

On the other hand, if you have met a woman that you genuinely feel you could eventually see yourself entering into a long-term, emotionally profound, strictly monogamous (or even polyamorous) romantic relationship with … or even more so, you see yourself marrying this woman and raising children with this woman … then take time to '**vet**' her properly in order to make sure that she does not fall into the category of the women that I discussed and described in the last five chapters of this book.

Stop allowing your intense fascination with a woman's physical beauty and sex appeal to cloud your judgment and cause you to be so easily manipulated by women or to cause you to confuse "true love" with mere *infatuation*.

A woman being exceptionally beautiful and incredibly sexy should never be used as the sole and specific criteria for a woman becoming your next long-term girlfriend or future wife. If all you want from a woman is a few episodes of short-term casual sex, then there is nothing wrong with you emphasizing nothing more than a woman's looks and sex appeal (unless the woman is a clear

*Psycho Bitch* type who might begin stalking you if you decide to leave her alone and ignore her indefinitely).

When you are in the market for a long-term girlfriend and future fiancée and wife, a woman's moral character and integrity is **extremely important**. You want a woman that is honest, down-to-earth, easy to get along with, very feminine, and **genuinely cares about you as a human being**.

Much love and respect to everyone who supports all of my writings and teachings and adheres to the knowledge and wisdom I choose to share with the general public and the entire world.

**Mooooooooooooode Ooooooooooooone Baby.**

**Go out in the world and make great things happen for you.**

Good luck in your search for 'true love' and sexual satisfaction my friend.

# About Author Alan Roger Currie

Alan Roger Currie was born and raised in Gary, Indiana and graduated from Wirt High School in the Miller Beach neighborhood of Gary.

Later, Currie matriculated at Indiana University, in Bloomington, Indiana, where he graduated with a Bachelor of Arts degree with a major in Economics and a minor in Theatre & Drama and Psychology. Currie also completed one year of the Graduate Business (MBA) program in the Kelley School of Business. Currie has been a member of Kappa Alpha Psi fraternity since November 1982.

Beginning with 2006, Currie has been interviewed on national television, nationally syndicated broadcast radio, and he has been interviewed for a number of newspaper and magazine articles. Currie has been a featured speaker for many conferences and workshops both in the United States and internationally, and he conducts online consultation sessions (via Skype®) and One-on-One / Face-to-Face Coaching Sessions with hundreds of men worldwide.

Currie is married and has one son and resides in the Chicagoland region of the United States.

www.ingramcontent.com/pod-product-compliance
Lightning Source LLC
Chambersburg PA
CBHW031507270326
41930CB00006B/286
* 9 7 8 1 7 3 6 1 9 5 1 2 3 *